BRAIN TEASERS

SALLY MORGAN

ACKNOWLEDGMENTS

Publishing Director	Piers Pickard
Commissioning Editors	Jen Feroze, Catharine Robertson
Editor	Jacqueline McCann
Art Director	Andy Mansfield
Author	Sally Morgan
Designer	Kim Hankinson
Print production	Nigel Longuet
With thanks to:	Jennifer Dixon

STAY IN TOUCH
lonelyplanet.com/contact

Lonely Planet Offices

AUSTRALIA
The Malt Store, Level 3, 551 Swanston St., Carlton,
Victoria, 3053 Australia
T: 03 8379 8000

IRELAND
Digital Depot, Roe Lane (off Thomas St), Digital Hub, Dublin 8, D08 TCV4

USA
124 Linden St., Oakland, CA 94607
T: 510 250 6400

UK
240 Blackfriars Road, London, SE1 8NW
T: 020 3771 5100

Published in April 2018 by Lonely Planet Global Ltd
CRN: 554153
ISBN: 978 1 78701 315 5
www.lonelyplanetkids.com
© Lonely Planet 2018
Printed in Singapore

10 9 8 7 6 5 4 3 2

MIX
Paper from responsible sources
FSC™ C021741

Paper in this book is certified against the Forest Stewardship Council™ standards. FSC™ promotes environmentally responsible, socially beneficial and economically viable management of the world's forests.

BRAIN TEASERS

SALLY MORGAN

A brain teaser is a puzzle that gets your mind whirring and buzzing to the point where you'll forget you were ever bored! And that is why this book is perfect for any occasion in which boredom is likely to strike.

Whether you're on a long journey, lounging around at home on a rainy day, or waiting to be seen by the brain surgeon, these brain teasers are for you! They'll take your mind on a little journey all of its own. With these travel-themed puzzles, you and your brain will explore the world. But don't keep them all to yourself – put the whole family to the test!

When you're ready to see how you've scored, you'll find all the answers on pages 152–159.

ON THE MOVE

Complete these puzzles so that each row, column, and box of four squares contains just one of each of the following things you might see on the road.

1

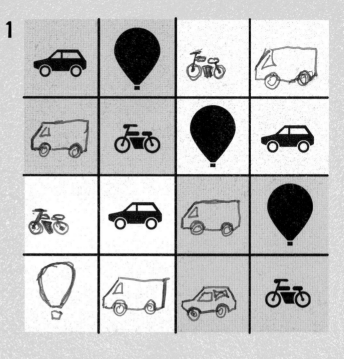

2

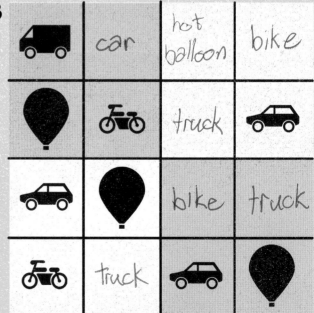

3

6

4

bike		car	truck
car			hot balloon
hot balloon	bike		car
		hot balloon	bike

5

bike			
	car		truck
truck			bike
car	bike	truck	

6

bike		car	truck
car			hot balloon
hot balloon	bike		car
		hot balloon	bike

7

bike			
	car		truck
truck			bike
car	bike	truck	

SCRAMBLED CITIES

So you think you know your capital cities? Unscramble the cities in the left column, then draw a line to connect each capital to the correct country!

1 rapis *paris*
2 teasdramm *amsterdam*
3 rinble *berlin*
4 racebran
5 hastingnow cd *washington dc*
6 orem *rome*
7 nongewltil
8 wen heldi *new dehli*
9 dramid *madrid*
10 jinbeig *beijing*
11 bosenu raies

6 Italy
1 France
9 Spain
2 Netherlands
8 India
10 China
5 US
Australia
3 Germany
New Zealand
Argentina

GRANDMA'S BIRTHDAY

Can you use logic to solve this puzzle?

It's Maya's grandma's birthday. Maya wants to visit her grandma's house on the island and prepare a surprise party before Grandma gets home from playing golf. Maya has a cake, Grandma's dog, Pickles, and her cat, Whiskers.

Only Maya can row the boat. The boat will only hold Maya and one other thing. The dog loves to eat cake so cannot be left alone with it. The cat loves to scratch the dog so those two can't be left alone together.

Can you figure out how to get Maya, the cake, Pickles, and Whiskers across to Grandma's house in as few trips as possible without the cake being eaten or the dog getting scratched?

READY FOR TAKE-OFF?

It's time to take to the skies with this air-travel word search. See if you can find all the words below on the opposite page. Look carefully – the words may be written horizontally, vertically, diagonally, or even backwards.

suitcase
carousel
departures
arrivals
check-in
pilot
terminal
backpack
gate

shops
restaurants
passport
plane
helicopter
taxi
runway
security

S	H	E	S	E	C	U	R	I	T	Y	B	M	Q	X	G
E	E	N	S	S	C	H	E	C	K	I	N	L	P	Z	L
R	L	S	W	A	T	D	R	L	A	N	I	M	R	E	T
U	I	K	H	L	C	N	M	C	W	D	R	N	R	N	R
T	C	W	N	O	B	T	A	J	G	Q	V	A	T	W	Y
R	O	N	Z	T	P	R	I	R	W	A	C	I	P	Y	D
A	P	L	X	W	O	S	D	U	U	K	T	N	X	T	Q
P	T	R	D	U	T	R	T	Y	S	A	B	E	S	A	L
E	E	Q	S	X	R	M	R	A	G	D	T	L	R	B	T
D	R	E	D	G	O	K	H	B	G	T	A	S	V	N	Z
M	L	K	D	D	P	K	R	D	V	V	T	K	E	J	N
P	N	M	R	Y	S	J	D	U	I	R	T	Y	M	R	D
L	V	R	N	D	S	T	R	R	N	O	R	R	M	B	R
A	G	L	T	L	A	Q	R	Q	L	W	D	T	Z	M	L
N	L	N	J	W	P	A	M	I	B	Q	A	J	N	M	T
E	W	T	B	A	C	K	P	A	C	K	D	Y	Y	T	Q

11

SAY WHAT YOU SEE!

Can you solve these brain-bending visual word puzzles? The first puzzle shows you how it's done. Good luck!

Example:

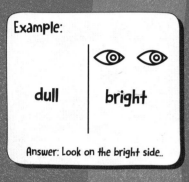

dull | bright

Answer: Look on the bright side..

1

OUINT

2

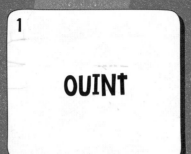

/ dog / dog /
cat cat cat

3

bend
backwards

4

 track

---

5

6

_____
read
_____

7

Look You Leap

8

P.M.
the town

9

ASPIINN

10

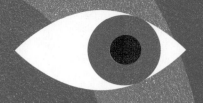

star

11

cut
the rest

12

13

rood

14

u
p
s
i
d
e

15

stood
mis

16

beat
beat bush beat
beat

17

fa   st

13

MORSE MADNESS

Morse code was invented as a way of sending written messages over long distances using short bursts of electricity along a wire. Each letter of the alphabet was given its own sequence of short and long pulses, otherwise known as dots and dashes. Look at the Morse code alphabet below, and see if you can decode the messages on the opposite page.

A •-	N -•	0 -----
B -•••	O ---	1 •----
C -•-•	P •--•	2 ••---
D -••	Q --•-	3 •••--
E •	R •-•	4 ••••-
F ••-•	S •••	5 •••••
G --•	T -	6 -••••
H ••••	U ••-	7 --•••
I ••	V •••-	8 ---••
J •---	W •--	9 ----•
K -•-	X -••-	
L •-••	Y -•--	? ••--••
M --	Z --••	

1 - /••••/• •--•/•-••/•-/-•/• •-••/•/•-/•••-/•/••• •-/- •----/••--- •--•/--

2 --/•/•/- --/• ••/-• •--•/---/--/•

3 ••••/•-/•••-/• •- --•/•-•/•/•-/- -/•-•/••/•--

4 •--/••••/•-/ -/••/•••/ -•--/---/••-/•-• -•/•-/--/• ••--••

You try it! Write your name in Morse code below.

--/•-/•-•/-•--

NUMBERS UP!

Figure out what comes next in these devilish sequences!

1.   1 3 5 7 9 *11 13 15*

2.   1 11 21 31 41 *51 61 71*

3.   1 6 11 16 21 *26 31 36*

4.   1 2 4 7 11 ... ...

5.   29 28 26 23 19 ... ...

6.   triangle square pentagon
....

7.   1 2 3 5 8 ... ...

8.   3 6 12 24 48 ... ...

9.   57 50 43 36 29 ... ...

10.   1 3 9 27 81 ... ...

MATH MAYHEM

Can you fill in the missing numbers and solve the
sequences? then practice adding to 21 – quickly!

top ten!

1 + <u>9</u> = 10
<u>2</u> + 8 = 10
<u>3</u> + 7 = 10
4 + <u>6</u> = 10
5 + <u>5</u> = 10
<u>6</u> + 4 = 10
<u>7</u> + 3 = 10
<u>8</u> + 2 = 10
9 + <u>1</u> = 10

twenty-one!

0 + 21 = 21
1 + <u>20</u> = 21
2 + <u>19</u> = 21
3 + <u>18</u> = 21
<u>4</u> + 17 = 21
5 + <u>16</u> = 21
<u>6</u> + 15 = 21
<u>7</u> + 14 = 21
8 + <u>13</u> = 21
<u>9</u> + 12 = 21
10 + <u>11</u> = 21

<u>11</u> + 10 = 21
<u>12</u> + <u>9</u> = 21
13 + <u>8</u> = 21
<u>14</u> + <u>7</u> = 21
<u>15</u> + <u>6</u> = 21
<u>16</u> + <u>5</u> = 21
17 + <u>4</u> = 21
<u>18</u> + <u>3</u> = 21
<u>19</u> + <u>2</u> = 21
<u>20</u> + <u>1</u> = 21
<u>21</u> + <u>0</u> = 21

SPIN THE WHEEL

These ferocious Ferris wheels will get your brain in a spin! Place a number on each pod. The sum of the pods next to each other must equal the sum of the pods opposite. We've done the first one for you!

Example:

$4 + 3 = 7$

$2 + 4 = 6$

$3 + 1 = 4$

4 3

2 1

2 5

$2 + 2 = 4$

$5 + 1 = 6$

$2 + 5 = 7$

Rules for riders

Use only numbers 1–6.

You can use a number twice.

1

2
5   3
4

2

3
4   2

3

6 2
3

18

MIND-BENDERS

These puzzles will have your brain spinning!

Who's speaking?

Johnny's mom has 4 children. Jimmy is the oldest. He's 11 and likes football most of all, followed by reading. Ella comes next; she's 8 and a half and loves to bake cakes and do puzzles! Then comes Conor. He's 5 and just started school. He loves dressing up as a superhero! The youngest is 4 and loves climbing trees and playing outside. What is his name?

R.I.P.

Why can't a man living in Scotland be buried in England?

Here comes the bride!

Why can't a woman in France marry her widower's brother?

Bucketloads

A man has two buckets. One holds 5 gallons of water and the other holds 3 gallons. How can he measure out 1 gallon of water without spilling any?

FLAGTASTIC

Look at the world flags below, then draw a line to connect them with the countries they represent. No peeking at the answers!

1.

2.

KENYA ⁵   SWITZERLAND ⁹   BRAZIL ⁷   JAPAN ⁸   CANADA ³

3.

4.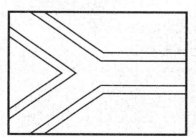

5.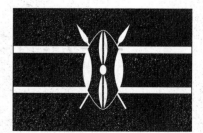

6.

7.

8.

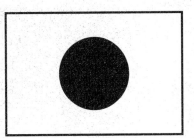

TURKEY¹   NEW ZEALAND¹⁰   NEPAL⁶   WALES²   SOUTH AFRICA⁴

9.

10.

21

NO SUCH PLACE?

Only one of the crazy place names below is made up – all of the others are real! Can you spot the fake?

Spiderman
Turkey

Mörön
Mongolia

Nasty
United Kingdom

Monster
Netherlands

Punkeydoodles Corners
Canada

Hell
Norway

Silly
Belgium

Eek
US

Banana
Australia

Nice
France

Hot Coffee
US

POLE POSITION

Get your thinking cap on and see if you can figure out
the answers to these two racing questions.

The flag goes down, and you're off! Things are looking
good, the finish line is in sight, and you just manage
to pass the car in second position. In what place
do you finish?

It's the second race of the day, but this one isn't going
too well. You manage to pass the last person at the
finish line. What position do you finish in this time?

AIRPORT SUDOKU

Complete the puzzles so that each row, column, and box of four squares contains just one of each of the following things you might see at an airport.

1

2

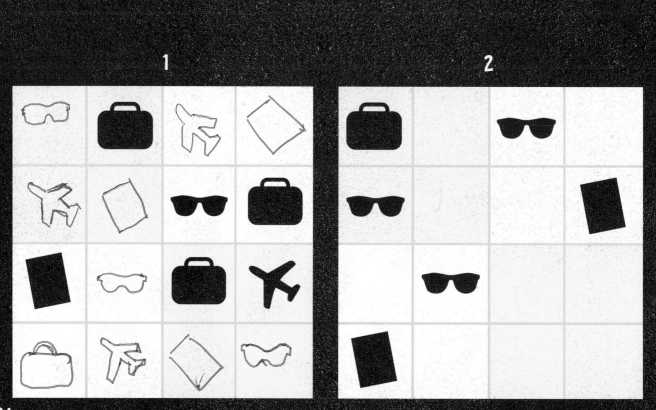

FLAG FINDER

Semaphore is a way of sending messages by holding flags in different positions. Red and yellow flags are used at sea to communicate over long distances. Use the semaphore alphabet here to decode the messages on the opposite page.
Can you spell out your name using your arms?

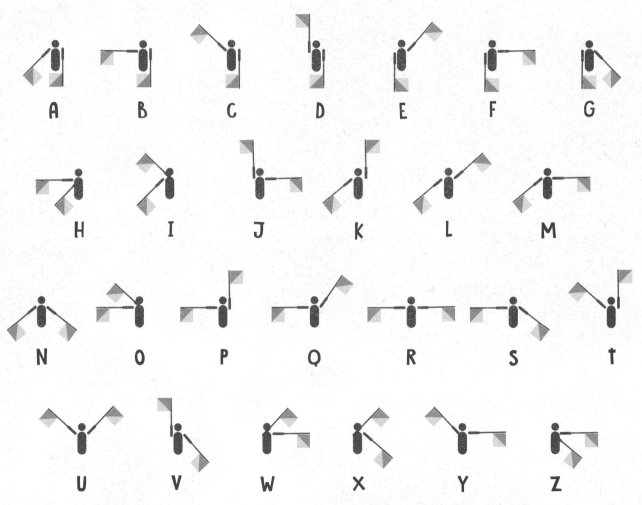

1

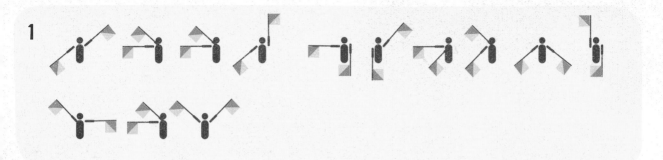

2

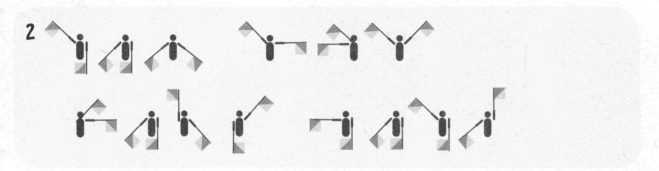

3

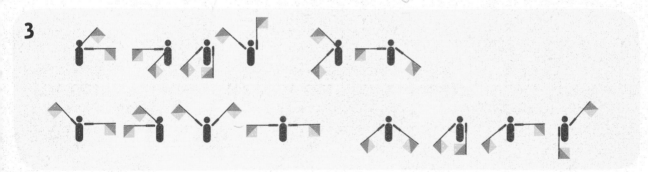

Write your name in semaphore here.

BIG-CITY QUIZ

How well do you know your cities? Let's put your knowledge to the test and see if you can match each city with its description. One city has two descriptions, can you tell which?

Kathmandu ✓   New York ✓   Cape Town ✓   Paris ✓   Beijing ✓

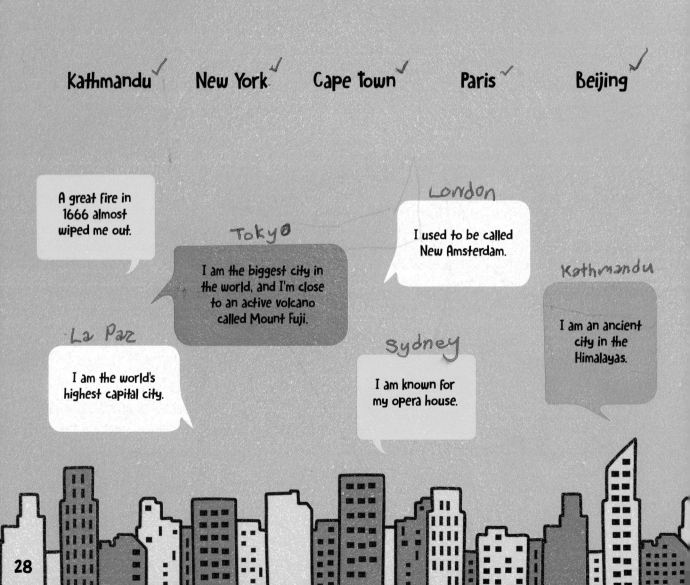

A great fire in 1666 almost wiped me out.

London
I used to be called New Amsterdam.

Tokyo
I am the biggest city in the world, and I'm close to an active volcano called Mount Fuji.

Kathmandu
I am an ancient city in the Himalayas.

La Paz
I am the world's highest capital city.

Sydney
I am known for my opera house.

28

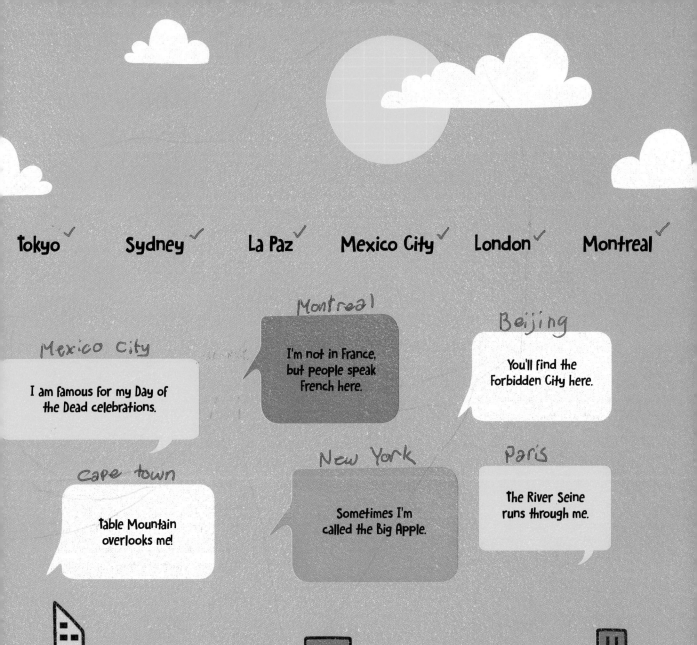

30

DOT TO DAKOTA

Connect the dots to discover a famous landmark in South Dakota, US. Can you name it, too?

FAMOUS PLACES

Can you guess the famous landmarks from these tricky puzzles?
Which one would you most like to visit?

1

G   D
R N
A

2

L
O
N
D
O
N

3

1:00 P.M.   2:00 P.M.   3:00 P.M.

12:00 P.M.   4:00 P.M.

11:00 P.M.   5:00 P.M.

10:00 P.M.   6:00 P.M.

9:00 P.M.   8:00 P.M.   7:00 P.M.

4

E
I
F
F
E
L

5

BEN

6

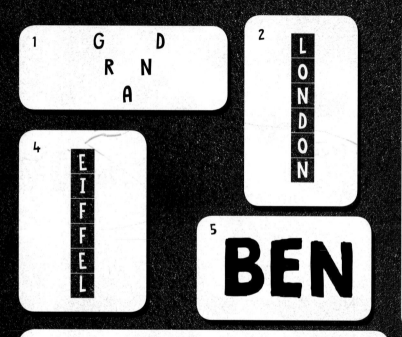

| CHINA | CHINA | CHINA | CHINA |

| CHINA | CHINA | CHINA |

| CHINA | CHINA | CHINA | CHINA |

| CHINA | CHINA | CHINA |

| CHINA | CHINA | CHINA | CHINA |

7

Sydney Harbour

8

GIZA
GIZA GIZA GIZA
GIZA GIZA GIZA GIZA GIZA
GIZA GIZA GIZA GIZA GIZA GIZA GIZA
GIZA GIZA GIZA GIZA GIZA GIZA GIZA GIZA
GIZA GIZA GIZA GIZA GIZA GIZA GIZA GIZA GIZA GIZA GIZA
GIZA GIZA GIZA GIZA GIZA GIZA GIZA GIZA GIZA GIZA GIZA GIZA GIZA
GIZA GIZA GIZA GIZA GIZA GIZA GIZA GIZA GIZA GIZA GIZA GIZA GIZA GIZA GIZA

9

PISA
PISA
PISA
PISA
PISA
PISA

10

Leicester[2]

11

M A R B L E
M · · · · E

12

A
M N
I J
L A
I R
K

13

Victoria

14

U N T A
O I
M N

ALL SQUARE

How many squares can you see in this picture?
There may be more than you think!

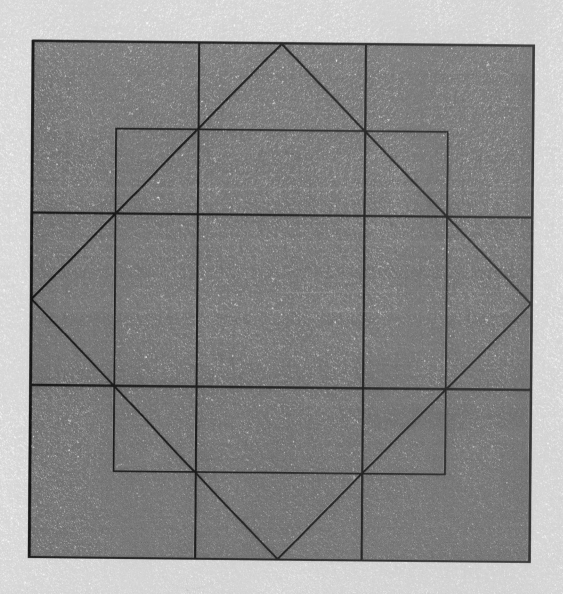

PUZZLE IN PIECES

One of these four boxes contains the pieces that make up the puzzle on the opposite page, but which one?

THE CURSE OF THE PYRAMIDS

In these puzzling pyramids, the number at the top is the sum of the two numbers below.

Example:

45

20 + 25

5 + 15 + 10

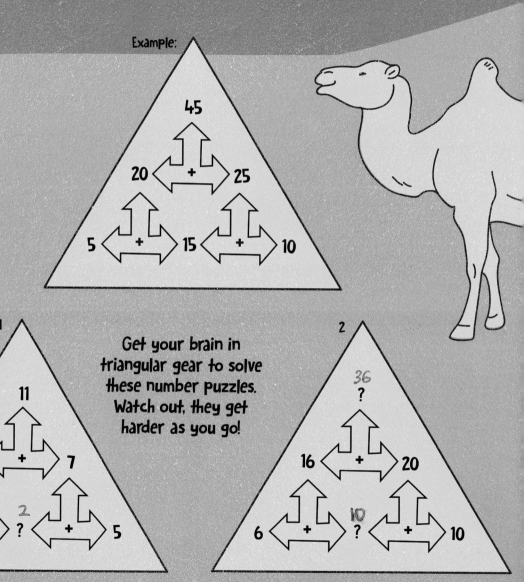

Get your brain in triangular gear to solve these number puzzles. Watch out, they get harder as you go!

1

11

4 + 7

2   2
? + ? + 5

2

36
?

16 + 20

            10
6 + ? + 10

RIDDLES OF THE SPHINX

The sphinx is a mythical creature of ancient Greece and Egypt, known for asking cryptic questions and riddles. It had the head of a human, the body of a lion, and sometimes the wings of a bird. Find out if you can wrap your head around these roar-some riddles!

1 What gets harder to catch the faster you run?

2 What has an eye but cannot see?

3 What starts with T and ends with T and only has T inside?

4 What goes up as rain comes down?

5 What has feet but no legs?

6 What has arms but no hands and helps you see?

7 What has two arms and four legs but no elbows?

8 What gets bigger the more you take away?

9 What has leaves but also a heart?

10 What has many branches but no leaves?

IT'S NO PICNIC!

Feeling hungry? Stop your tummy from rumbling with these seriously yummy sudoku puzzles.

Complete the puzzles so that each row, column, and box of four squares contains just one of each of the picnic items.

1

cupcake	sandwich	water bottle	apple
water bottle	apple	cupcake	sandwich
apple	water bottle	sandwich	cupcake
sandwich	cupcake	apple	water bottle

2

apple	water bottle	sandwich	cupcake
cupcake	sandwich	apple	water bottle
sandwich	cupcake	water bottle	apple
water bottle	apple	cupcake	sandwich

3

cupcake	sandwich	apple	water bottle
apple	water bottle	cupcake	sandwich
water bottle	cupcake	sandwich	apple
sandwich	apple	water bottle	cupcake

Are you ready for more of a challenge? Make sure each picnic box of six squares has only one of each of the items below. There should be only one item in each row and column, too.

chocolate bar

bag of chips

cupcake

apple

sandwich

water

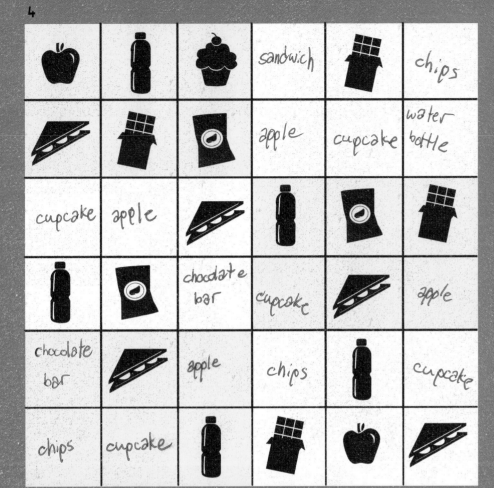

🍎	bottle	cupcake	sandwich	chocolate bar	chips
sandwich	chocolate bar	chips	apple	cupcake	water bottle
cupcake	apple	sandwich	bottle	chips	chocolate bar
bottle	chips	chocolate bar	cupcake	sandwich	apple
chocolate bar	sandwich	apple	chips	bottle	cupcake
chips	cupcake	bottle	chocolate bar	apple	sandwich

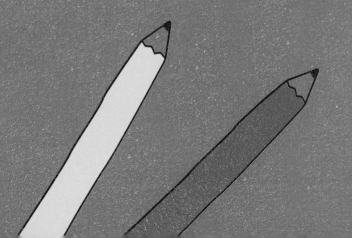

41

BUREAU DE CHANGE

Try out these brain-busting *bureau de change* problems. Can you use the exchange rate to figure out what you can buy in the souvenir shops?

EXCHANGE RATE €1 euro = $1.5 Canadian dollars (CAD)

If you change €20 into Canadian dollars, how many dollars will you have?

a $15
b $30
c $35

$10 CAD

How many moose mugs can you buy?

$15 CAD

How many bottles of maple syrup can you buy?

If you change $75 into euros, how many euros will you have?

a €100
b €50
c €25

€5

How many Eiffel tower snow globes can you buy?

€10

How many boxes of Belgian chocolates can you buy?

ALL SPENT

Keep your mind on the money, and match up each country with the correct currency!

Thailand   Krone

United Kingdom   Dollar

France   Ringgit

US   Yuan

India   Baht

Norway   Yen

Ireland   Euro

Malaysia   Pound sterling

Japan   Rand

China   Euro

Turkey   Rupee

South Africa   Lira

LOST IN THE DARK

Crawl through this dark, bat-infested cavern and make your way to the cool waterfall at the exit!

Start here

Finish

Q What is the first thing that
bats learn at school?

A The alphabat!

45

HIT THE HIGHWAY!

Find all of the items below in this on-the-road word search. The words may be written horizontally, vertically, diagonally, or even backwards.

car	fire engine	power lines
truck	ambulance	horizon
van	horse trailer	accident
lamp post	tree	road sign
restaurant	plane	tow truck
camper van	roadwork	junction
motorcycle	traffic jam	
police car	breakdown	

46

h f t r a f f i c j a m z q r
o i a n a v r e p m a c b p h
r r l m k s t n e d i c c a r
s e a z b y k l g m y z k a t
e e m t d u y r o i p v c l g
t n p d n x l t o o s e d b y
r g p v m a o a w w c d r k n
a i o j t r r e n i d e a o t
i n s n c o r u l c a a i o n
l e t y o l w o a k e t o o r
e j c j i v p t d t c e z r t
r l t n c l a o r n s i r r m
e n e n a v w r u u r e u t p
z s y n r n r j a o c c r t g
j y e y l y k z h c k k l q l

47

WHEEL OF FORTUNE

Can you crack the code using the wheel of fortune? To decode the messages, find each letter on the inner wheel and write down the corresponding letter on the outer wheel. The first message has been decoded for you. Good luck!

FX JFXD FX FGH

(as easy as abc)

1   N XUD BNYM RD QNYYQJ JDJ

I SPY WITH MY LITTLE EYE

2   N'R LTNSL FWTZSI NS HNWHQJX

I'M GOING AROUND IN CIRCLES

3   MTSJXYD NX YMJ GJXY UTQNHD

HONESTY IS THE BEST POLICY

‒‒‒ ‒‒‒‒‒‒ ‒‒ ‒‒‒ ‒‒‒

4   BMFY NX DTZW SFRJ?

WHAT IS YOUR NAME?

48

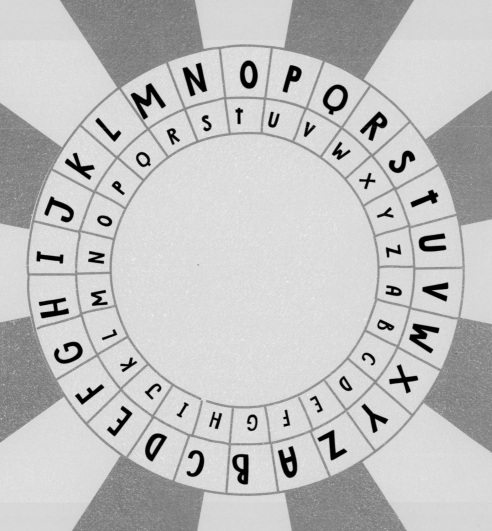

Now use the wheel to write your name in code.

RFWD

WARNING — HAZARD AHEAD!

Watch out, these tricky questions will really fry your brain!
When you've given it a go, try them out on your friends.

1 Which of these statements is correct?

Nine and nine is sixteen
or
Nine and nine are sixteen

2 Unscramble these two words to make just one word.

jousted wonder

3 Which four days of the week start with the letter T?

4 Anna has two cats, a dog, and three rabbits. Maeve has one cat, three dogs, and a canary.

How many of Anna's pets could say they were the same animal as Maeve's?

5 Last year, I was flying a plane with 256 passengers from London to Sydney, Australia.

In Dubai, 56 passengers got off the plane and 50 new passengers boarded. In Sydney, all the passengers got off the plane and 256 new passengers boarded. On the flight home, 200 passengers got off the plane in Dubai and 76 boarded the plane to London.

In London, all of the passengers got off the plane.

What was the name of the pilot?

6 How many legs does a butterfly have if you call its antennae legs?

7 You are in a cold, dark cabin with a wood stove, a fireplace, and a candle. You have only one match left. What must you light first?

8 How many colored pencils do I have if none are purple and all but three are green, all but three are pink, all but three are orange, and all but three are blue?

9 What was the first gift you were given? It is yours but is mostly used by others.

10 You have a bucket filled to the brim with sand. It is very heavy. What can you put in your bucket that will make it lighter and easier to carry?

11 Mr. Marco Mason met Miss Marion Morgan on a mudflat in the Mississippi.

How many *ms* are there in my sentence?

12 What is so delicate that uttering just one word will break it?

13 Would you rather have a venomous snake bite you or a ferocious tiger?

14 If four cockerels lay two eggs a day for six days, how many eggs would you have on the seventh day?

WORD SCRAMBLE

Look at the groups of words below. Can you figure out
which two in each group are the odd ones out?

1

lemon

grape

(leek)

fig

lime

(lettuce)

2

(ostrich)

parrot

blackbird

robin

heron

(penguin)

3

marker

(sharpener)

pen

pencil

crayon

(ruler)

4

(Canada)

Not in

Italy

Sweden

Not countries

(Amsterdam)

Europe

(Australia)

(Madrid)

5

angry

(happy)

upset

sad

(content)

annoyed

AMUSEMENT PARK ATTRACTION

Are you amazing at anagrams? How many words of four letters or more can you build out of each of the central words in these Ferris wheels? Write each new word in one of the pods.

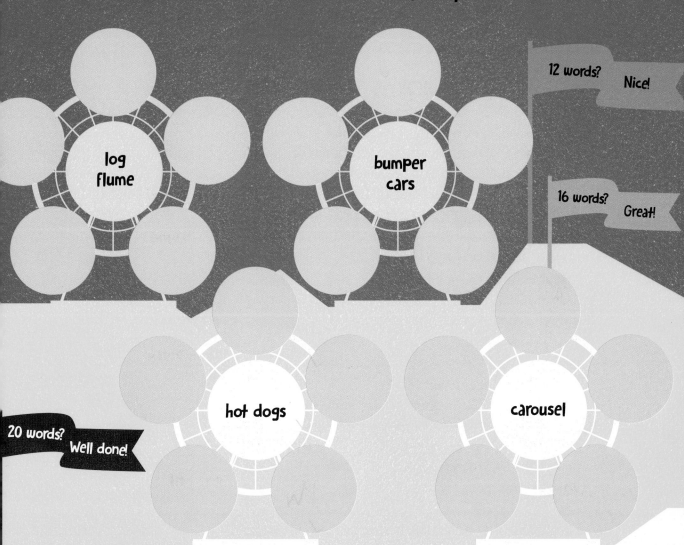

log
flume

bumper
cars

12 words?   Nice!

16 words?   Great!

hot dogs

carousel

20 words?
Well done!

SAFARI CROSSWORD

Solve the clues to reveal some of the awesome
sights you might see on safari.

ACROSS

4   Fake-teared, water-loving reptile with a big bite (9)
6   The biggest danger to endangered animals (7)
10   Prowls on the savannah, not in the jungle (4)
11   Black and white but no two are alike (5)
12   Never forgot being called big ears (8)
14   Keeps tourists and the animals safe (4, 6)
15   Fastest animal on Earth (7)
17   Insect with an itchy bite (8)

DOWN

1   Pitch your tent here for the night (4)
2   Long-necked leaf-lover (7)
3   Loves mud and wallowing a-lot-amus (12)
5   Black or white with a nose of horn (10)
7   Safari vehicle (4)
8   Small deer that runs very fast (7)
9   Animals stop here for a drink (5, 4)
13   Covered in spots it can't change (7)
16   Laughs at other animals' leftovers (5)

1. CAMP
2. GIRAFFE
3. HIPPOPOTAMUS
4. CROCODILE
5. RHINOCEROS
6. GAZELLE (scribbled)
7. JEEP
8. GAZELLE
9. WATERHOLE
10. LION
11. ZEBRA
12. ELEPHANT
13. LEOPARD
14. PARK RANGER
15. CHEETAH
16. HYENA
17. MOSQUITO

WHERE ON EARTH?

Can you put each of these countries in the correct continent? Write the letter beside each country in the circle of the continent to which it belongs.

a Morocco ✓
b Spain ✓
c Belgium ✓
d Thailand ✓
e Kenya ✓
f Brazil ✓
g Argentina ✓
h China ✓
i Canada ✓
j United States of America ✓
k New Zealand ✓
l Fiji ✓
m Peru ✓
n Czech Republic ✓
o India ✓
p Tanzania ✓

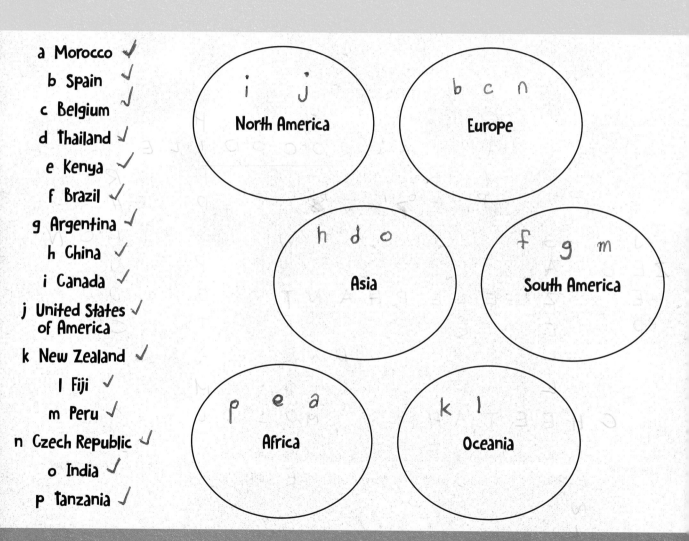

North America: i j

Europe: b c n

Asia: h d o

South America: f g m

Africa: p e a

Oceania: k l

Which of these is the seventh continent?   1. Arctic   2. Antarctica

IN THE BAG!

Study the contents of the suitcase below for 30 seconds. Try to remember all the items inside. After 30 seconds, turn the page and follow the instructions. No peeking!

STILL IN THE BAG...

Look closely at the picture of the suitcase below. Can you spot which six items are missing? Do you notice anything different about the suitcase itself?

NAME THAT HABITAT

Reveal the habitats lost in these word puzzles!

1 ground
cave

2

r t
/ / /
o s
/ /
f e

3
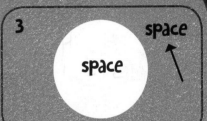
space
space

4
w
a
t
e
r

5 H$_2$O LAND

6 POOL

8 tree tree tree tree tree tree tree tree

7 sea sea sea sea sea sea sea sea sea sea

9
R
A   C
C   t
I

UNDERSEA SCRAMBLE

Find your way through the shipwreck from start to finish.
Write down all the letters that you pass, then unscramble
them to discover what lies beneath the wreck!

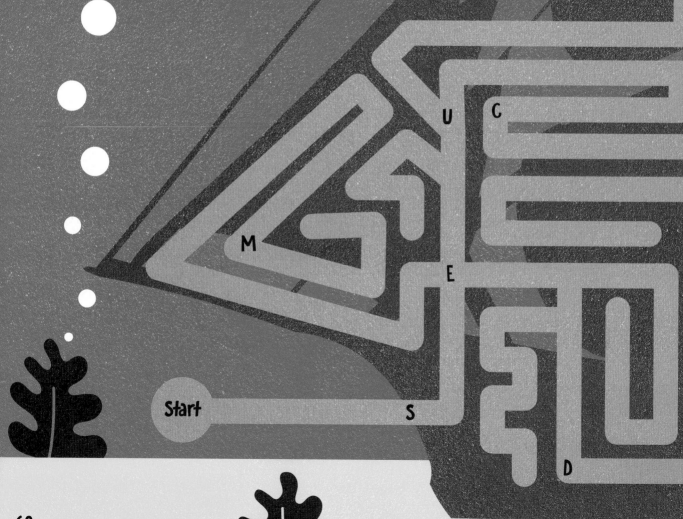

U

G

M

E

Start

S

D

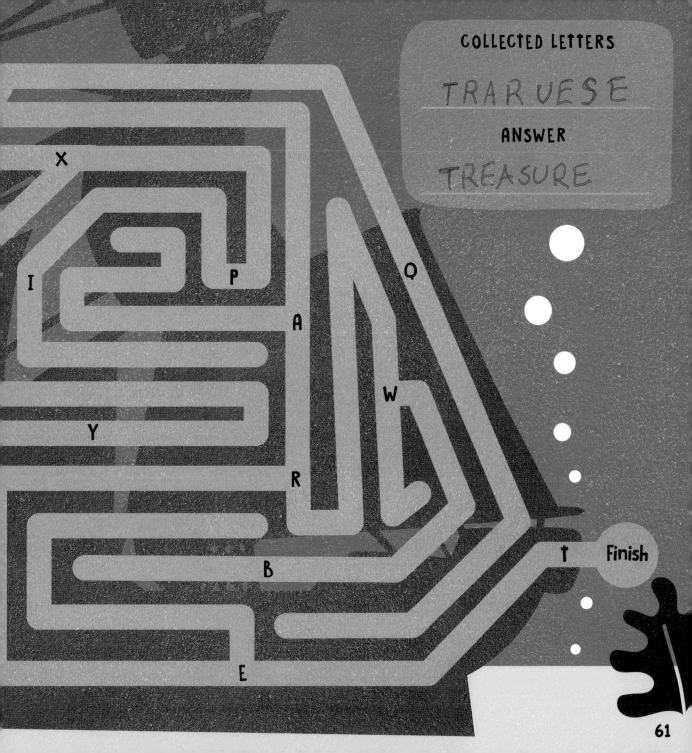

COLLECTED LETTERS

TRARUESE

ANSWER

TREASURE

X

I

P

Q

A

W

Y

R

B

t Finish

E

SPORTING SAY WHAT YOU SEE!

Get the adrenaline pumping by finding the extreme sports behind these brain-boggling word puzzles.

1

nis nis nis nis
nis nis nis nis
nis nis

2

s
  k
    i
      i
        n
          g

3

twelve inches

4

~~country~~
skiing

5

j   u   m   p

6

meters meters meters meters meters meters meters
meters meters meters meters meters meters meters
meters meters meters meters meters meters meters
meters meters meters meters meters meters meters
meters meters meters meters meters meters meters
meters meters meters meters meters meters meters
meters meters meters meters meters meters meters
meters meters meters meters meters meters meters
meters meters meters meters meters meters meters
meters meters meters meters meters meters meters
meters meters meters meters meters meters meters
meters meters meters meters meters meters meters
meters meters

7

 ing

8

AB

9

n
  i
  a
  t
n
u
 o
m

10

SWIMMING

11

jumpjumpjump

12

>jump<

jump   jump

BRAIN WORKOUT

Paul, Joe, Maisie, and Zack are good skiers. Paul is 7 years old. Joe is 3 years older than Zack and 2 years younger than Maisie. Zack is 3 years older than Paul. How old is Maisie?

WHERE AM I?

Can you unravel these twisted clues to reveal the countries they refer to?
The first destination has been completed for you!

Here's an example:

My third isn't in fume but stars in fame. (a)
My last is in eat but not in hat. (e)
My first is in leaf but not in leave. (f)
My second is in breath but not in bathe. (r)
My fifth is in back and also in clout. (c)
My fourth is the second in sneak and snout. (n)

Where are you? FRANCE

1

My third is in pain but not in pin.
My second is fourth in can't.
My first is third in slide.
My last is third in why.
My fourth appears twice in fallen.

– – – – –

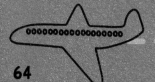

2

My first three are what happens when you can't not.
My fourth and my sixth are the same as my second.
My fifth is in bed and also in and.

_ _ _ _ _ _

3

My sixth is first in last.
My second is in pray but not in pay.
My first is in able but not in ale.
My third and fourth begin the alphabet and close it out.
My fifth is second in pin.

_ _ _ _ _ _

4

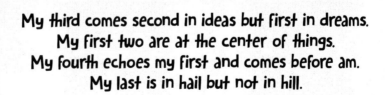

My third comes second in ideas but first in dreams.
My first two are at the center of things.
My fourth echoes my first and comes before am.
My last is in hail but not in hill.

_ _ _ _ _

THE TAJ MAHAL

Kai wants to buy two identical Taj Mahal statues for his bookshelf at home. Only two of these nine statues are identical. Can you figure out which ones?

THE TAJ MAHAL MISHAP

Oh no! Kai dropped one of the statues! Can you circle the pieces of the statue that make up the picture so that he can put it back together?

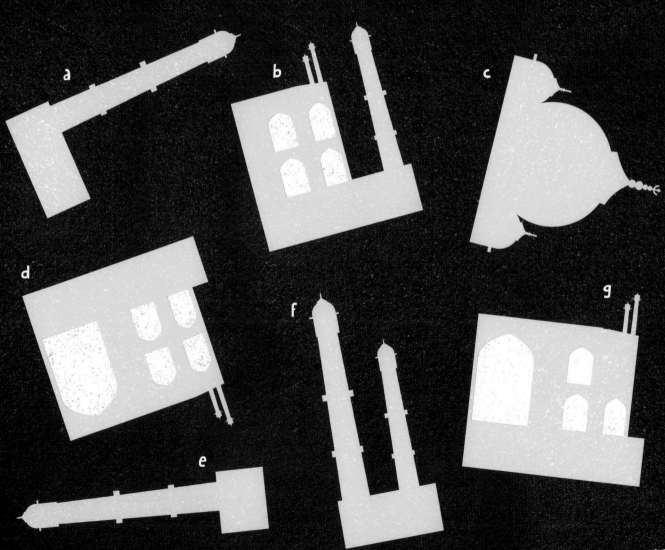

CRAZY BAGGAGE CAROUSEL

Four passengers have lost their bags. Can you help them identify their suitcases? Circle the pieces of luggage that best fit each passenger's description.

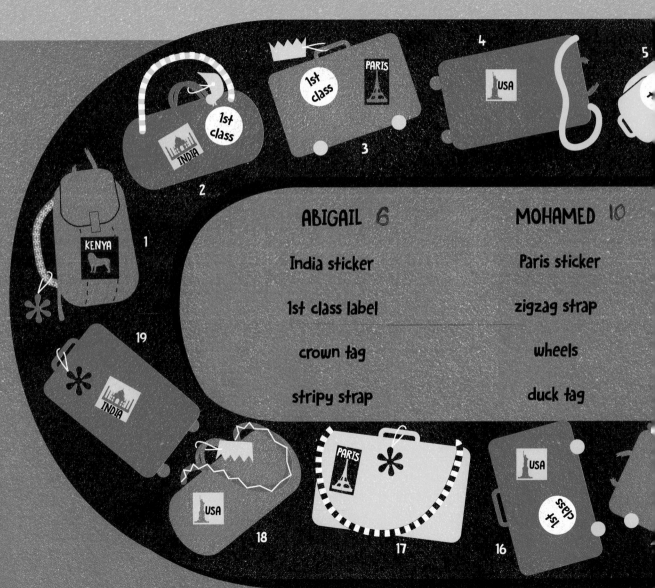

ABIGAIL 6

India sticker

1st class label

crown tag

stripy strap

MOHAMED 10

Paris sticker

zigzag strap

wheels

duck tag

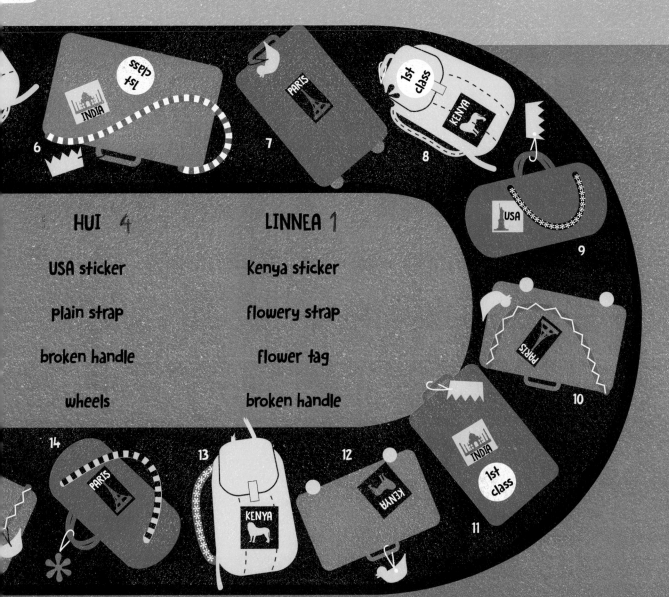

HUI 4

USA sticker

plain strap

broken handle

wheels

LINNEA 1

Kenya sticker

flowery strap

flower tag

broken handle

TANGLED CHUTES

Follow the tangled waterslides to discover which rider falls into which pool.

Pirate's Plunge

a 3   c 4

Coral Lagoon

b

2 d

THEY DO THAT THERE?

People do some pretty crazy things around the world in the name of sports and culture! Can you spot which of the events listed on the map are real and which are fake?

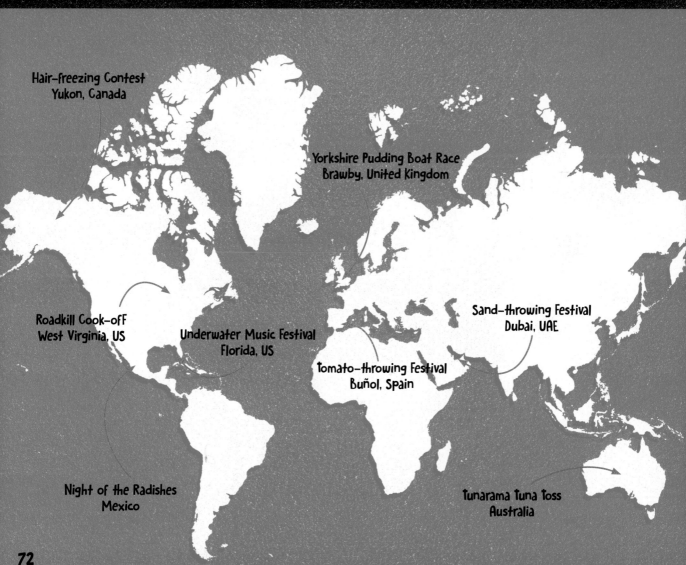

Hair-freezing Contest
Yukon, Canada

Yorkshire Pudding Boat Race
Brawby, United Kingdom

Roadkill Cook-off
West Virginia, US

Underwater Music Festival
Florida, US

Sand-throwing Festival
Dubai, UAE

Tomato-throwing Festival
Buñol, Spain

Night of the Radishes
Mexico

Tunarama Tuna Toss
Australia

DANCING PARTNERS

The left column contains scrambled country names, and the right shows names of dances that have got in a muddle. Can you unscramble everything and match each dance with the country it comes from?

1 earningat

2 tarisua

3 whaiia

4 zirbla

5 nipas

6 coldsant

a calfomen

b natog

c mbasa

d luah

e alihghdn dincang

f zlwta

ROLL THE DICE

These dice contain three hidden four-letter words from the natural world. Can you figure out what each one is by combining one letter from each die? You can only use each letter once, so if you choose T from die number one for your first word, you can't use it again in words two or three. Good luck!

1 _____

2 _____

Now combine the letters on all of the dice and see how many new words you can make.

10 words or more = not bad
20 words or more = some serious skills
30 words or more = you're a word wizard!

3 _____

MATCH PLAY

Add, move, and remove matches to solve these sticky situations.

1. Remove one match to make this sum add up.

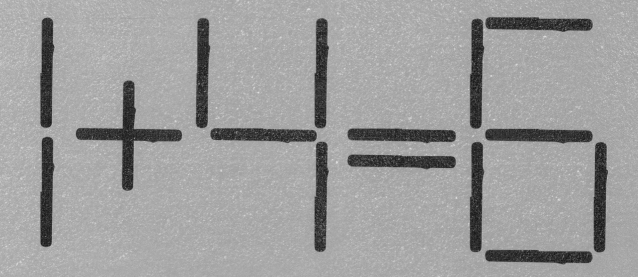

1+4=5

2. Can you move three matches to leave three squares?

3. Move one match to turn the horse to face another direction.

RUNE READER

Before the invention of the Latin alphabet, which formed the basis of many European languages, some places in Europe wrote with symbols called runes. Check them out!

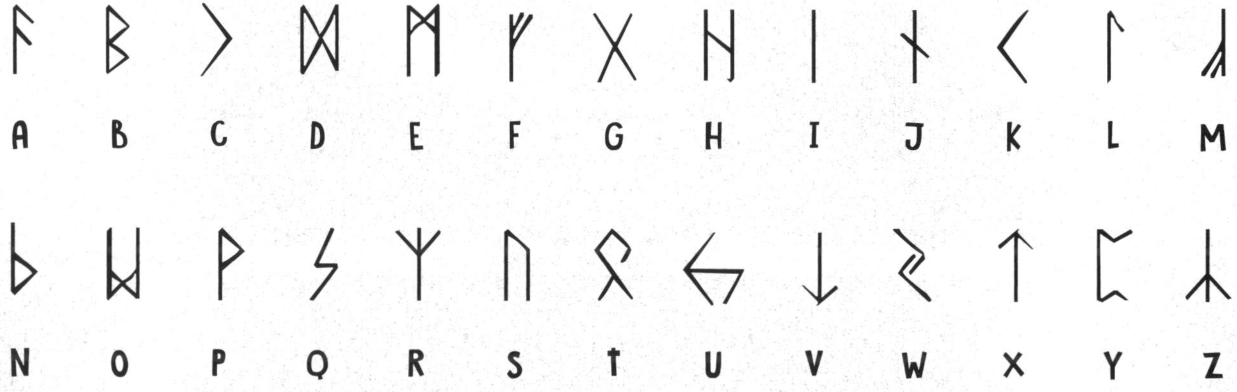
A B C D E F G H I J K L M
N O P Q R S T U V W X Y Z

Can you use the key above to figure out what these ancient inscriptions say?

1

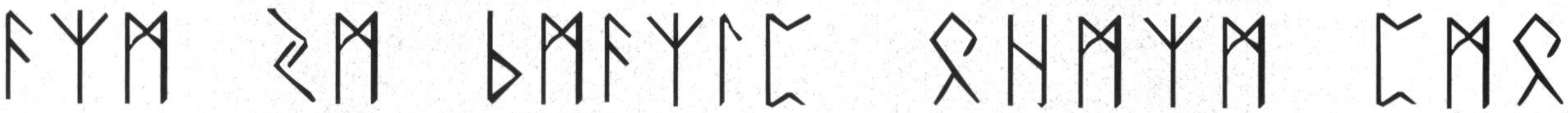

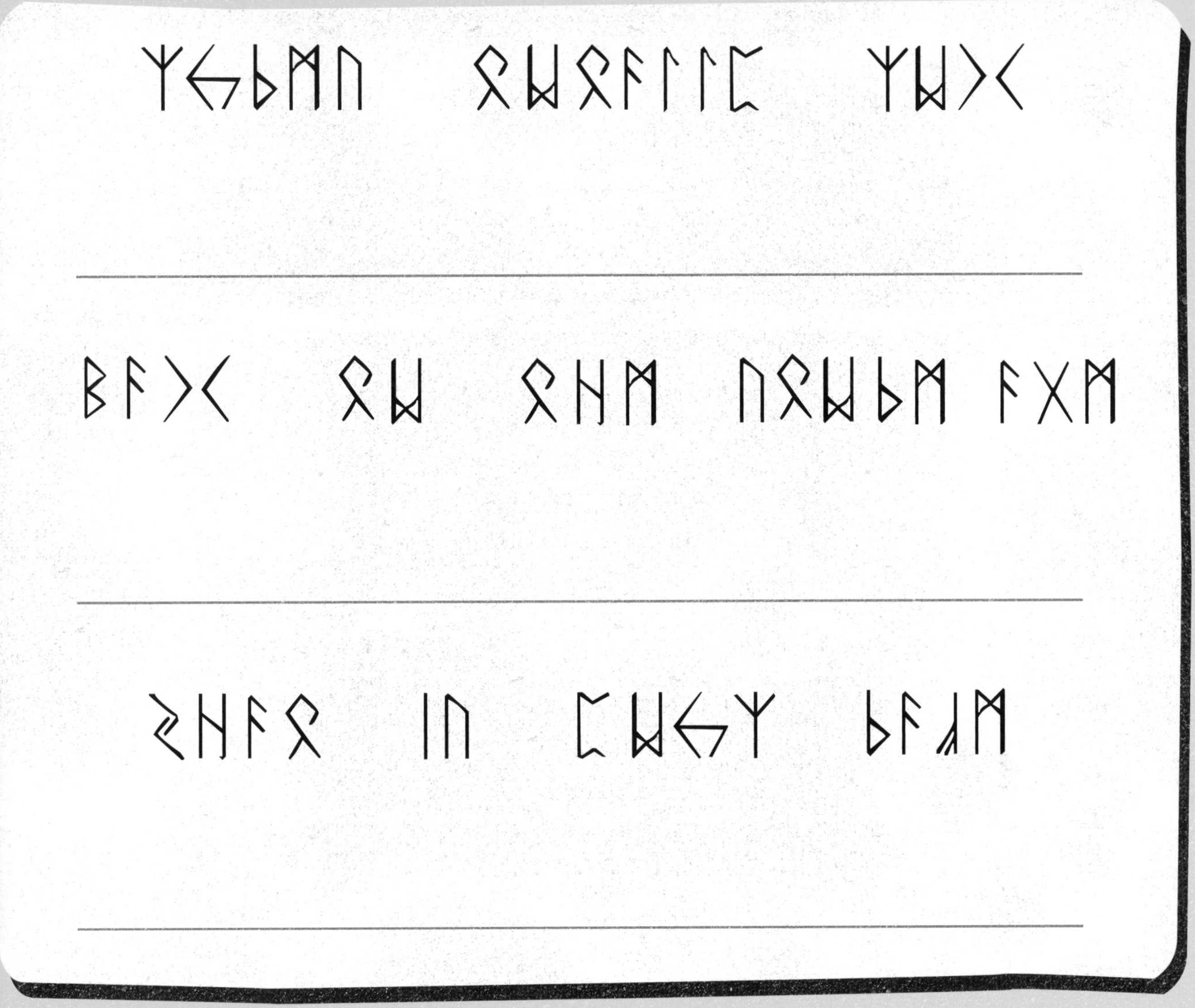

ᚣᛖᚦᚻᚢ   ᚱᚢᚱᚠᛚᛚᚳ   ᚣᚹᚷᚳ

ᛒᚠᚷᚳ   ᚱᚹ   ᚱᚻᛗ   ᚾᚱᚹᚻᛗ   ᚠᚷᛗ

ᛋᚻᚾᚱ   ᛁᚾ   ᚳᚹᚷᚣ   ᛒᚠᚦᛗ

Write your answer to question 4 in runes here:

MOVING HOME

Magnus has built a log cabin on his desert island, but has just realized that he built it facing the wrong way! Can you move one log to make his cabin face in the other direction?

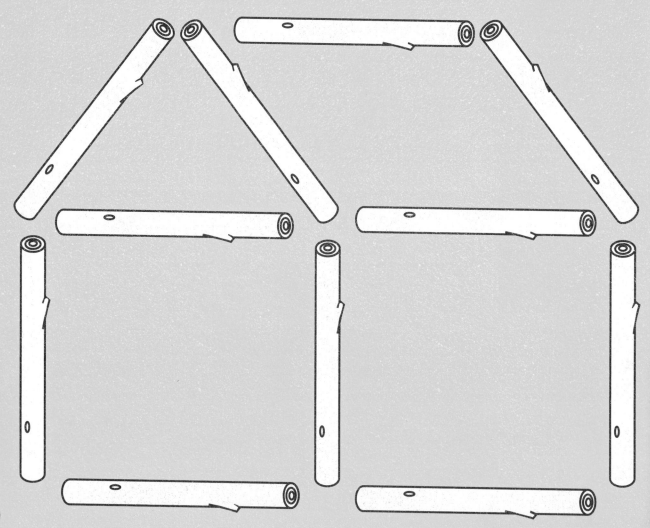

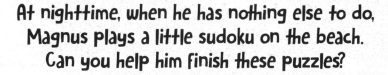

DESERT ISLAND SUDOKU

At nighttime, when he has nothing else to do,
Magnus plays a little sudoku on the beach.
Can you help him finish these puzzles?

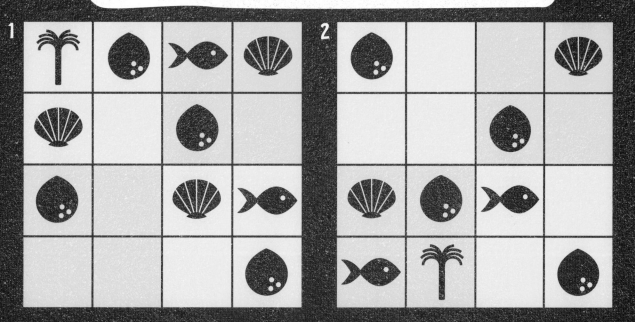

SWING THROUGH THE THREES

Color all the boxes containing numbers that are multiples of three. Who's that hiding in the trees?

BEACH-BAG MIX UP

The Murphys are all packed and ready for the beach! Study their beach-bag for 30 seconds, then turn the page and follow the instructions.

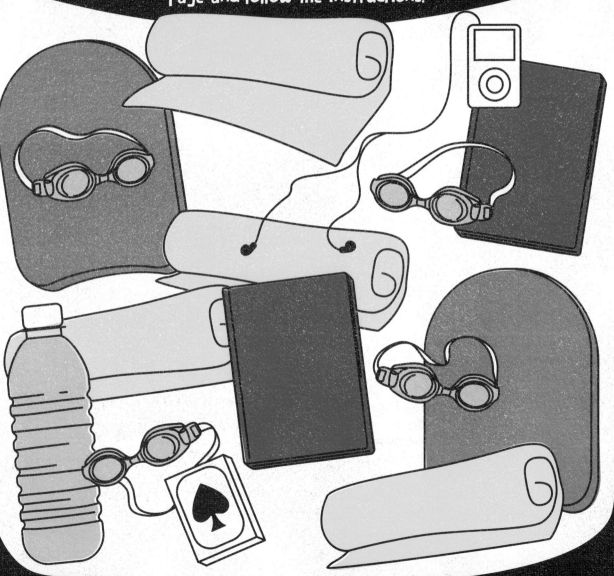

Oh no! Mr. Murphy dropped the beach-bag on the way home, and everything fell out! Can you tell which four items he left behind and which two items he picked up that do not belong to the family?

TRICKY TRIANGLES

A) How many triangles can you see in this shape?

B) And how many triangles can you see in this shape?

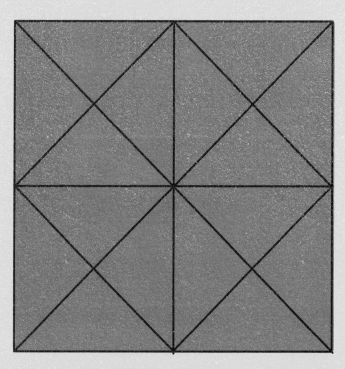

AMUSEMENT PARK FUN!

Find your way through the amusement park and note the letters you pick up on the way. Unscramble them to reveal the newest attraction.

start

x

g

g

o

l

a

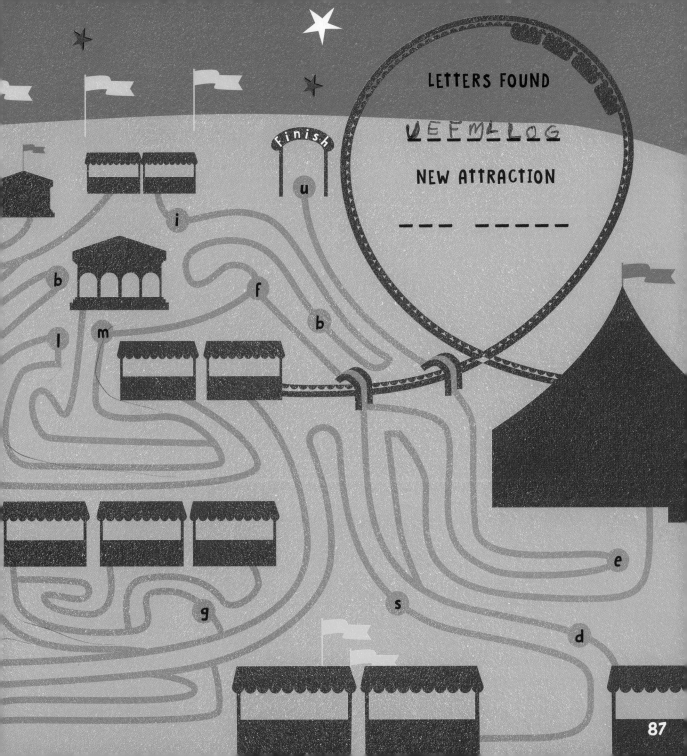

LETTERS FOUND

U E F M L L O G

NEW ATTRACTION

_ _ _   _ _ _ _ _

THINKING CAPS ON!

Find the well-known words and phrases behind these visual word puzzles!

1

cycle
cycle
cycle

_____

2

121

_____

3

Jack

_____

4

✓ ets

_____

5

LOST

word
word
word
word

_____

6

TRAFstuckFIC

_____

7 kcap

_____

8 roads roads

_____

9 Where? Here.

_____

10 YOUbetweenME

_____

11 on theworld

_____

12 ground
feet
feet
feet
feet
feet
feet

_____

13  the world

_____

BLINDING BLIZZARD

Yikes! It's a snowstorm!
Shade in all the shapes with two
dots in them to find out who's been
left out in the cold.

91

PASSPORT PHOTO MYSTERY

Harrison, Jacob, James, and David all left their passport photographs at the photo studio. Can you play detective and match the owner with the picture from the descriptions given?

HARRISON _b_	JACOB _g_	JAMES _i_	DAVID _h_
light hair	dark hair	bald	light hair
glasses	beard	glasses	mustache
beard	mustache	beard	no glasses

a

b

c

d

e

f

g

h

i

j

k

93

AROUND-THE-WORLD RIDDLES

Want to keep your friends and family guessing?
Try these head-scratching riddles!

1 What runs all around a country but doesn't move?

2 What has a key that can't open any doors?

4 What gets wetter as it dries?

5 The more of me you take, the more you leave behind. What am I?

3 What can you see only once in a year, twice in a week, but never in a day?

6 Why do polar bears never eat penguins in the wild?

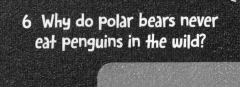

7 I run but never walk. I have a mouth but never talk. I have a bed but never sleep. I have a bank but no money to keep. What am I?

8 What do you throw away when you need it and bring back when you don't?

10 What weighs more: a pound of confetti or a pound of potatoes?

9 What travels all over the world but stays in the corner?

LOOKING FOR WILDLIFE

Can you find the animals in these wicked word puzzles?

1

 FISH

_____

2

>butter<

butter   butter

_____

3

D   D   D
    D   D
E   E   E
    E   E
E   E   E
    E   E
R   R   R
    R   R

_____

4

get down!

_____

5

1st place: ger
1st place: ger

_____

6

C

O

N

_____

7

SE STICK Ct

_____

8

pig pig pig

_____

9

SHARK

_____

10

north

bear

south

_____

11

puss puss puss puss
puss puss puss puss

_____

12

can
can

_____

13

mce mce mce

_____

14

rus	rus	rus	
	rus	rus	rus
rus	rus	rus	
	rus	rus	rus
rus	rus	rus	

_____

BE AN ARCTIC EXPLORER!

Use the clues below to help you complete the crossword opposite. The answers are all things you might see on an expedition to the Arctic.

ACROSS

3 Large sheet of ice (7)
4 Marine mammal hunted by polar bear (4)
6 This animal's coat turns white in winter (6, 3)
11 Ferocious white creature of the north (5, 4)
12 The top of the world (5, 4)
13 Blue and green spectacle in the night sky (8, 6)

DOWN

1 Unicorn of the sea (7)
2 Country closest to the North Pole (6)
5 Ship for smashing through the frozen ocean (10)
7 Frozen mountain floating at sea (7)
8 No nighttime in summertime (8, 3)
9 Many whales love to eat these (5)
10 Use this to find north (7)
14 All you need for a white Christmas (4)

HEAD SCRATCHER!

What do you
call 50 penguins in
the Arctic?

TREASURE ISLAND

Can you dig in the right spot and find the treasure?
Read the directions very carefully.

The treasure was buried beneath the sand.
It was buried at least one mile from the ocean.
It is buried at the same latitude (row) as two swamps
and the same longitude (column) as two forests.

Draw an X to
mark the spot.

KEY

swamp   forest

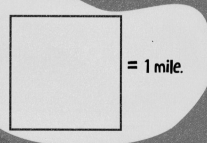

= 1 mile.

Lines of longitude

Lines of latitude

HIEROGLYPHS

The people of Ancient Egypt used an alphabet made up of small pictures called hieroglyphs. Can you use the hieroglyphic-style alphabet below to decode the ancient inscriptions opposite?

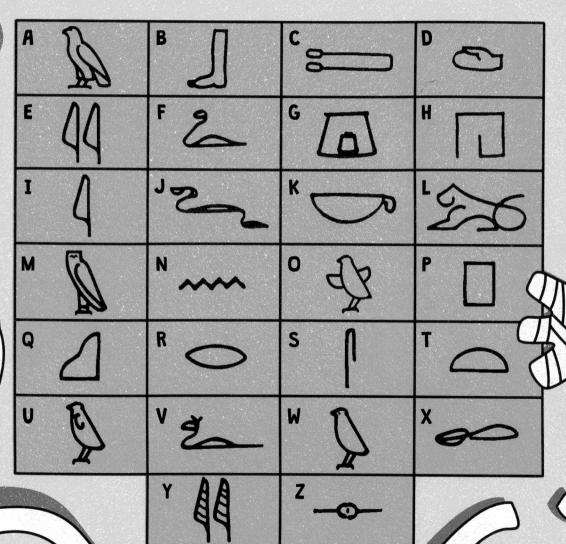

1

2

try writing your name in hieroglyphs.

MUDDLED MONUMENTS

Unscramble these famous landmarks and then connect them to the country where they can be found.

yensdy brarohu	US
wtero fo dolnon	Egypt
atsuet fo bretily	Russia
cluesmoos	United Kingdom
jta hmala	Greece
retag lalw	Italy
der requas	India
hornetnap	China
dripyams	Australia

SORT THE SOUVENIRS

Oh no! the souvenir shop at the Eiffel tower is a mess. Can you figure out which of the puzzle boxes below contains all the pieces that will make up the Eiffel tower on the left?

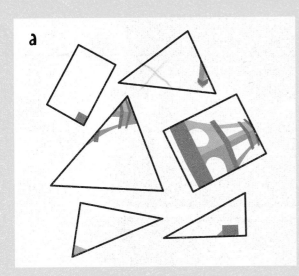

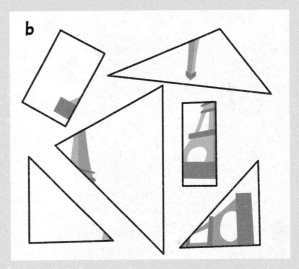

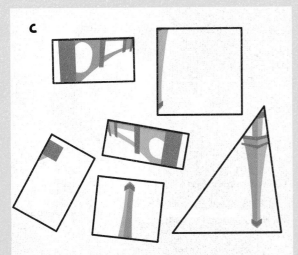

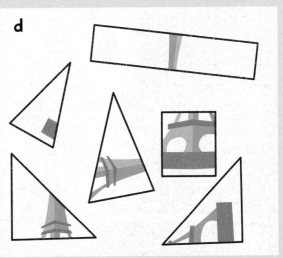

SCORCHING HOT!

Try this sizzling word search, and you'll find the things you may need if you visit the desert, and creatures you might see there. The words may be written forwards, backwards, up, down, or diagonally!

water bottle	scorpion	sand
tent	oasis	beetle
sun hat	backpack	gazelle
sunscreen	lizard	tumbleweed
camel	snake	salamander
cactus	spider	
dune	vulture	

n	e	e	r	c	s	n	u	s	d	l	z	d
k	c	a	p	k	c	a	b	s	j	v	n	t
e	k	w	x	o	m	e	u	y	l	a	u	t
r	v	a	r	r	a	n	k	e	s	m	v	s
u	s	t	g	e	h	s	m	a	b	l	c	t
t	u	e	q	a	d	a	i	l	n	o	m	e
l	t	r	t	d	c	n	e	s	r	s	l	b
u	c	b	e	q	r	w	a	p	t	l	l	r
v	a	o	m	l	e	a	i	m	e	n	e	b
m	c	t	d	e	t	o	z	z	a	d	d	t
z	k	t	d	u	n	e	a	i	i	l	n	t
k	y	l	r	d	n	g	e	p	l	e	a	q
b	w	e	l	w	p	e	s	b	t	n	l	s

PICTURE PLACES

Can you guess where these people are going from their cryptic picture messages?

5

6

7

1 LB.

8

109

IN THE LOOP

Each of these circles represents something people like to do on vacation. The area where two circles overlap shows where a person likes both activities. If three circles overlap, then all three activities are popular!

Avery likes the water and fancy food but doesn't like sand or sightseeing.

James likes water sports, eating out, and seeing the sights but doesn't like lying on the beach.

Ethan likes lying on the beach, exploring new places, and eating out, but doesn't like getting wet.

Chantal likes being active in the water, fine dining, and sightseeing but doesn't like lying on the beach.

Gloria loves eating out, preferably while she's sightseeing!

Shannon loves to lie on the beach.

Write each person's name in the circle that best represents what they like do.

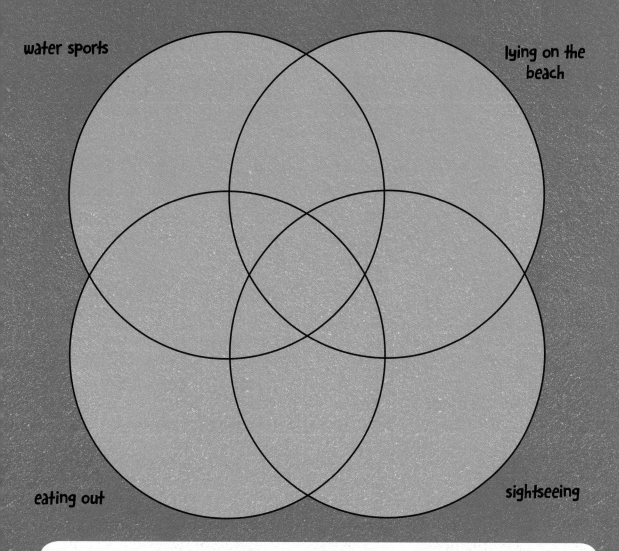

water sports

lying on the beach

eating out

sightseeing

Which people are most likely to have a fun time together?

VACATION TIME?

Try this mind-boggling vacation conundrum. Are you ready?

Joe is going on vacation and he's really excited! His friends Olivia and Tobias want to know when he's going, but Joe decides to keep them guessing. Figure out when Joe is going on vacation using this information:

Joe gives his friends these dates:

May 15   May 16   May 19

June 17   June 18

July 14   July 16

August 14   August 15   August 17

Joe tells Olivia the month of his flight, and he tells Tobias the day of his flight (neither Olivia nor Tobias hear what Joe says to the other one).

Olivia says, "I don't know when Joe is leaving, but I know that Tobias doesn't know either."

Tobias says, "At first, I didn't know when Joe was going on vacation, but now I do!"

Then Olivia says, "Now I also know when Joe is going on vacation."

When is Joe going? Use the space on the right to figure out the answer!

Hint: It helps to write out the information and think very carefully about what each person knows after each statement!

Olivia

May
June
July
August

Tobias

14
15
16
17
18
19

NOW YOU SEE IT

Connect the dots to reveal an ancient wonder!

Sometime between the years 500 BC and AD 500, the people of the Nazca Desert in Peru carved enormous pictures, called geoglyphs, into the ground. Many of these pictures can only be seen from the air and nobody is sure why the Nazca people made them.

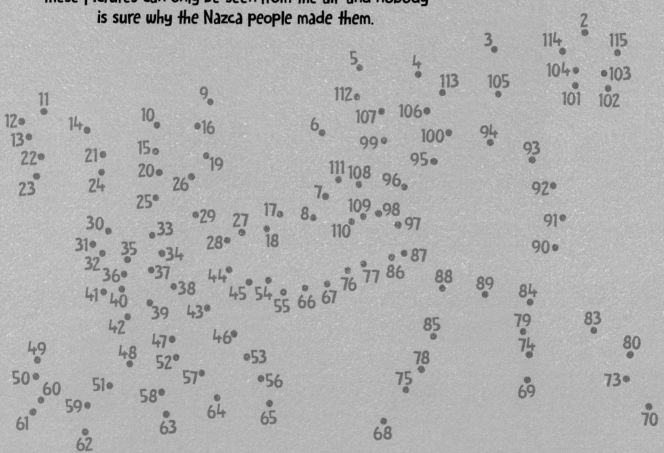

TRICKY TALES!

Can you untie these tricky tales?

1. A Canadian Mountie rode into town on Tuesday and stayed for five days but left on Tuesday. How can this be possible?

2. What is of little use unless it is broken?

3. A man in Delhi did not sleep for over 365 days. How did he do it?

4. Which weighs more: a ton of chocolate or a ton of balloons?

5. Two fathers and two sons went ice-skating and they all rented skates. Only three pairs of skates were rented. How is this possible?

6. If there are 15 oranges and you take three, how many do you have?

7. A man fell down a three-story staircase but didn't get hurt. How is this possible?

IT'S ALL GREEK

Greece is home to many ancient temples. How many triangles, squares, and rectangles can you spot in this one?

triangles

4

squares

16

rectangles

23

MENU MADNESS

Oh no! The menu signs at the International Food Festival are in a muddle! Can you match each dish to the country it comes from?

sushi	Hungary
moussaka	US
adobo	Italy
haggis	England
hamburger	Ireland
poutine	Jamaica
jollof rice	Thailand
roast beef	Scotland
goulash	Japan
Irish stew	Greece
ackee and saltfish	Canada
spaghetti	Philippines
pad thai	Ghana

FUNKY FOOD?

One of the best things about visiting new places is trying out new local dishes! Can you guess which of these delicacies are real and which we've made up?

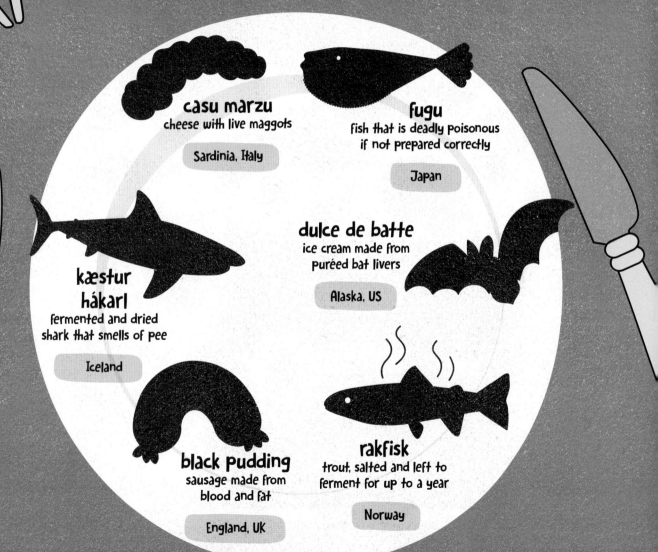

casu marzu
cheese with live maggots

Sardinia, Italy

fugu
fish that is deadly poisonous if not prepared correctly

Japan

dulce de batte
ice cream made from puréed bat livers

Alaska, US

kæstur hákarl
fermented and dried shark that smells of pee

Iceland

black pudding
sausage made from blood and fat

England, UK

rakfisk
trout, salted and left to ferment for up to a year

Norway

IN THE DEEP END

Here are a few more questions to tease your brain.
Try them yourself and then torment your friends!

1 Before the discovery of Mt. Everest, what was the highest mountain on Earth?

2 Rosie has five new hamsters. She named the first Red, the second Orange, the third Yellow, and the fourth Blue. What is the name of the fifth hamster.

3 What holds more water when it has more holes in it?

4 What can you take and hold but not touch with your hands?

5 What are the next two letters in this sequence?
W, A, T, N, T, L, I, ...

6 Ava has 18 stick insects. She gives away all but six of them. How many are left?

7 A little boy and a soldier in uniform are in the park. The boy is the soldier's son, but the soldier in uniform is not the little boy's father. How can this be?

8 What thrives when you feed it but fades when you water it?

9 What tree does everyone carry in their hand?

10 What is easy to catch but hard to throw?

SCORCHING SEQUENCES!

Can you solve these sequences and see them through to the end?
They may not be as hard as they look!

1

What comes next?

J F M A M J J A S O _ _

Hint: Don't take all year!

Is it?

a N, D
b J, M
c S, Z

2

Fill in the 'blank'.

Brazil, Lithuania, Australia, Norway, _____

Hint: It's right in front of you.

Is it?

a Sweden
b France
c Kenya

Which country comes next?

3

Ireland, UK, Holland, Germany, _____

Hint: Are you heading in the right direction?

Is it?

a Spain
b Italy
c Poland

What are the next two letters in the sequence?

4

R O Y G B _ _

Hint: You might find a pot of gold at the end of this.

Is it?

a L, R
b I, V
c E, R

What are the next three letters in the sequence?

5

O T T F F S S E _ _ _

Hint: We knew we could count on you.

Is it?

a N, T, E
b E, R, R
c E, N, N

BUSY BEACH

Can you find your way across the busy beach to the ice-cream truck? Write down the letters you collect on your way and rearrange them to reveal a yummy ice-cream flavor!

Start

123

wrybarters
ice-cream flavor
Strawberry

yum yum!

r

z

t

a

Finish

p

e

i

r

s

s

h

r

MONSTER MYSTERIES

Are you brave enough to take on these
spine-tingling picture challenges?

1

ALIVE

2

FOOT

3

the ~~dead~~

4

HORSEMHN

5

DEAD

↑

LIVE   LIVE

8

BLOOD WATER

6

Wicked
Witch

Wicked
Witch

Wicked
Witch

Wicked
Witch

9

FRIDAYFRIDAYFRIDAY
FRIDAYFRIDAYFRIDAY
FRIDAYFRIDAYFRIDAY
FRIDAYFRIDAYFRIDAY
→ FRIDAY

7

corpse
----
my

PERFECT PAIR

Two of the vases in this shop are identical.
Can you spot which ones?

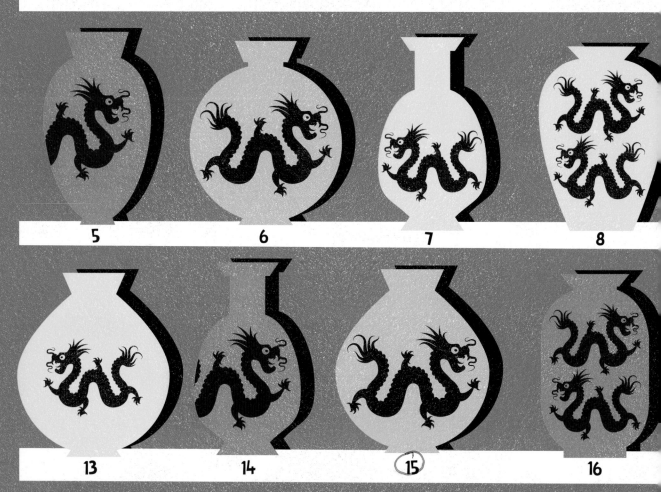

5

6

7

8

13

14

15

16

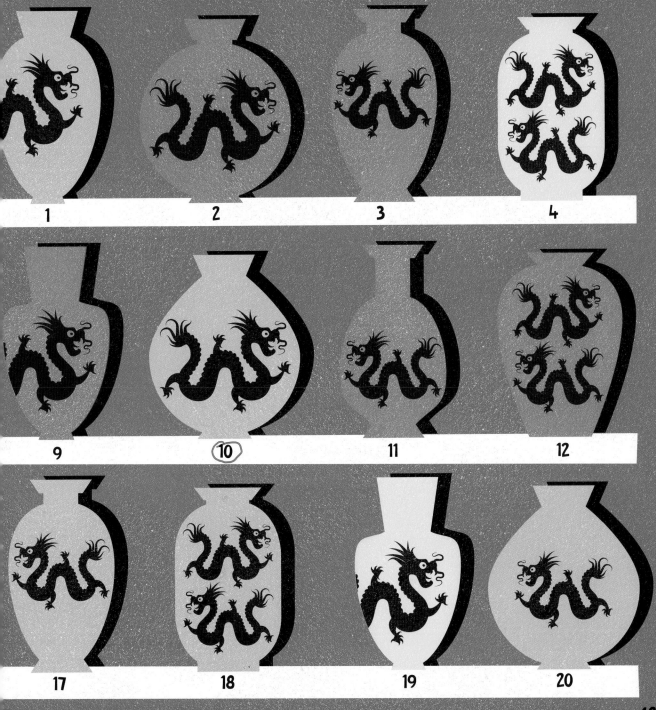

1

2

3

4

9

(10)

11

12

17

18

19

20

PYRAMID PILEUP

Can you figure out the missing numbers in the pyramid?
We've filled in a few numbers to help you get started.

Hint:
Numbers beside each other add up to the number directly above!

85

40   45

17   23   22

7   10   13   9

4   3   7   6   3

3   1   2   5   1   2

SECRET OF THE SPHINX

Try this sudoku and see if you can fit the word SPHINX into the grid. The letters must appear only once in each row, column, and block of six squares!

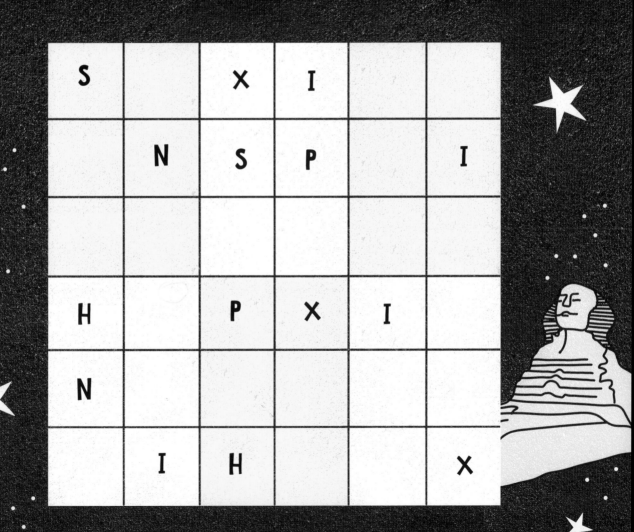

SQUARED UP

How many squares can you see in this picture?

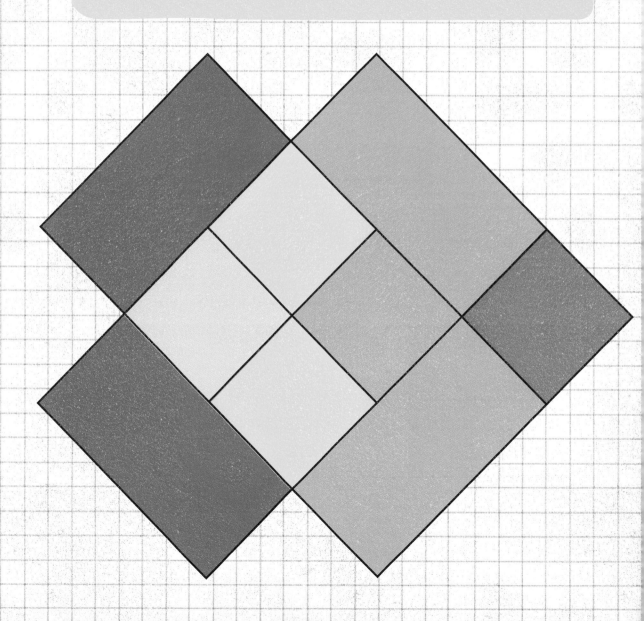

IN THE BOX

Which one of the boxes below contains all the pieces you need to make a square?

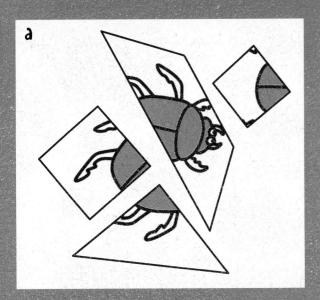

a

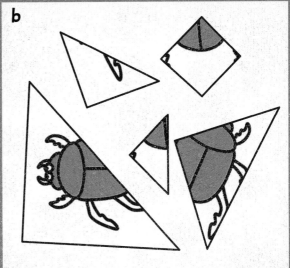

b

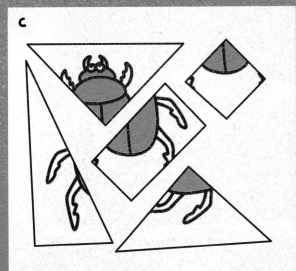

c

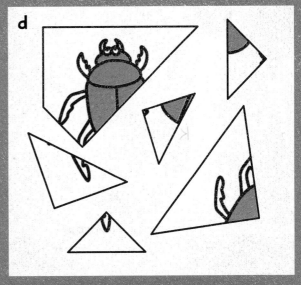

d

CAMPSITE CAPER

Can you help these four campers figure out where they are staying from the descriptions of their tents below?

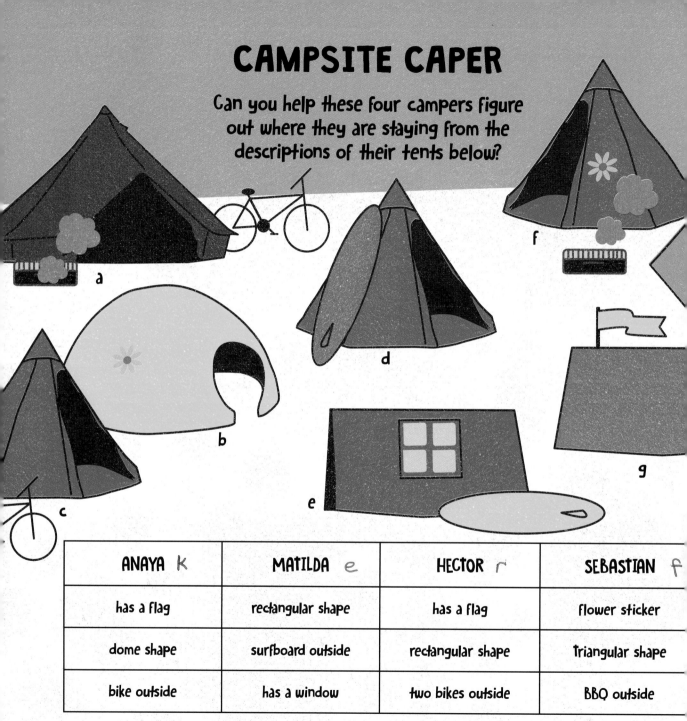

ANAYA k	MATILDA e	HECTOR r	SEBASTIAN f
has a flag	rectangular shape	has a flag	flower sticker
dome shape	surfboard outside	rectangular shape	triangular shape
bike outside	has a window	two bikes outside	BBQ outside

h

i

j

k

l

m

n

o

p

q

r

135

CAMPSITE SUDOKU

Make sure this campsite has all the right facilities by filling in the puzzle correctly. Each row, column, and block of six boxes must contain one of each of the facilities!

Facilities

showers

toilets

kitchen

tent

campfire

pool

1

2

LOST IN THE RAINFOREST

Lurking in the deepest, darkest corners of this word search are things associated with the Amazon Rainforest. Can you find them? You know the routine, so get going!

mahogany	tarantula	otter	electric eel
toucan	macaw	spider monkey	centipede
sloth	fig tree	manatee	bull shark
piranha	black caiman	heron	boa
poison arrow frog	pink dolphin	ant	viper
parakeet	crocodile	anaconda	capybara

```
t p a r a b y p a c p i r a n h a
o x o p i n k d o l p h i n a s d
u r z i m p x t e l e m d l p q y
c t m v s q m d l l y j u i j t w
a v t a y o e t e g n t d y m m y
n n l w h p n c z j n e m a c a w
n g d f i o t a m a r r b w d r t
t w k t i r g a r m d l e x w e v
n e n b i g o a o r a n z t l r g
e e e c u b t n n c o z o i t y z
c e e k d l k r k y h w d c j o b
s e t m a e l c e e y o f m a j l
l l q a y r a s r e c b v r r n y
t w o p n i a o h o b m i n o z a
w n n t m a n p r a w y p y v g l
y w a a h d m c y l r l e y d j r
r w n d d z m d v m g k r j w n g
```

5¢ .55

10¢ .50

25¢ 2.50

$1 15

MONEY MATTERS

Check out the piggy bank - it's full! Count the number of each type of coin inside. Then figure out how much money there is in the piggy bank in total!

$18.55

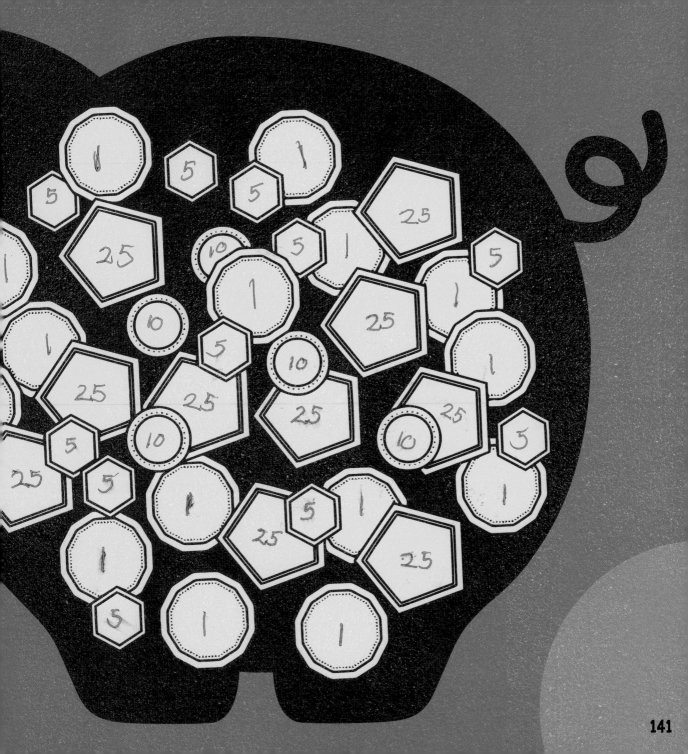

BIG-CITY CROSSWORD

Solve the clues to complete the crossword with some of the sights you might see in a big international city.

ACROSS

4   All sorts of fancy things are sold here (10, 5)
7   What happens when there are too many cars on the road (7, 3)
12 Sit down here and enjoy delicious food (10)
13 Get your cash here (4)
16 Red and green, stop and go (7, 5)
17 Where things are sold from stalls (6)
18 Catch your flight here (7)
19 A place to see beautiful paintings and sculptures (7)
20 Buy your stamps here (4, 6)
22 People who visit the city to see the sights (8)
23 Gray bird that loves the city (6)
24 Come here for a quick drink and a snack (4)

DOWN

1   Green space with swings and slides (4)
2   Learn about all kinds of history here (6)
3   Pay for a room and spend the night here (5)
5   Where to go when you are lost or need to report a crime (6, 7)
6   Leave your vehicle here (6)
8   A rail-y great place to go to when you want to avoid using a car (5, 7)
9   A fine place to borrow a book (7)
10 Flows through the city (5)
11 A royal family may live here (6)
14 Great place to see a play or a musical (7)
15 Where you go if you are injured or ill (8)
21 Settle down to watch a movie here (6)

HOW WAS YOUR JOURNEY?

Four friends are going on vacation, but they're all traveling by different modes of transport. Use the clues to figure out how each one gets there.

1 Karl's vehicle has wheels.

2 Rosa and Ian travel on land.

3 Bert loves the sea.

4 Ian brings a map for the journey.

	CAR	TRAIN	PLANE	BOAT
Karl			✓	
Rosa		✓		
Ian	✓			
Bert				✓

The friends have packed sandwiches for the journey and they each have something different. Read these clues to find out what each of them has!

1 Rosa and Bert are vegetarian.

2 Ian doesn't like poultry or avocados.

3 Karl does not eat fish.

4 Bert is allergic to dairy.

	TURKEY	CHEESE	TUNA	AVOCADO
Karl	✓			
Rosa		✓		
Ian			✓	
Bert				✓

LOST HABITATS

Can you muddle through the twisted clues to reveal the lost habitats?

1
My fourth is first in dark and drake.
My last is third in shark and shake.
My second is first in umbrella.
My first is sixth in storyteller.
My fifth is fourth in fourth.
My third is first in north.

2
My third is in beat but not in bat.
My fourth opens the alphabet.
My second is in fact but not in fat.
My first is last in hello.
My last is in tone but not in toe.

3
My first is third in bad
but fourth in trade.
My fifth is second in
art but first in raid.
My second and fourth
are in feast but not fast.
My third is not in pat but in past.
First in tiger and tape
in me come last.

4
My fourth is second and fifth in leaves.
My first is last in thief but not in thieves.
My third is last in four and floor.
My second is third in shoe and shore.
My last is at the start of trees.
My fifth opens and closes seas.

Write your answers here.

1 _ _ _ _ _ _

2 _ _ _ _ _

3 _ _ _ _ _ _

4 _ _ _ _ _ _

SUPER-SHAPE SUDOKU

Can you use your super sudoku skills to complete the puzzle? Make sure each row, column, and block of nine boxes contains only one of each symbol.

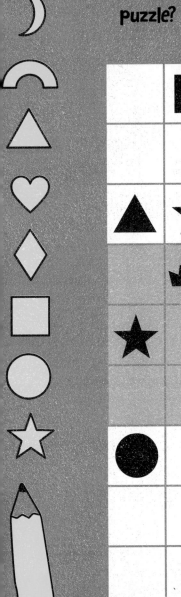

DITLOIDS

A ditloid is a puzzle that uses numbers and letters to make phrases. Can you figure out what these phrases mean?

1   7 D in a W

2   7 C of the R

3   7 C on E

4   60 S in a M

5   60 M in an H

6   24 H in a D

7   8 P in the SS

8   52 C in a P

9   12 M in a Y

10   26 L in the A

Here's an examp[le]

365 D in a Y

means
365 days in a yea[r]

22 1 46 P

70

L

11   5 F on a H

12   2 W on a B

13   3 W on a t

14   4 W on a C

15   6 S on a D

16   366 D in a LY

17   100 Y in a C

18   12 I in a F

19   10 t on your 2 F

20   360 D in a C

AT THE AMUSEMENT PARK

Four friends went to buy an ice cream and all chose something different. Follow the clues to find out what each one had.

1 Leo and Teddy like fruit.

2 Annie loves chocolate but doesn't like nuts.

3 Leo is allergic to strawberries.

4 Lily doesn't like fruit.

	strawberry	orange	pistachio	chocolate
Annie				✓
Leo		✓		
Lily			✓	
Teddy	✓			

After their ice cream, the four friends went on different rides in the amusement park. Read the clues to find out who went on what!

	carousel	ghost train	bumper cars	roller-coaster
Annie			✓	
Leo	✓			
Lily		✓		
Teddy				✓

1 Annie's favorite thing is driving!

2 Lily and Leo don't like heights.

3 Lily likes being scared but doesn't like spinning around.

4 Teddy loves heights and going fast.

ANSWERS

P6-7 ON THE MOVE

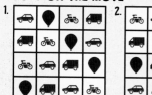

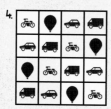

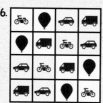

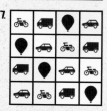

P8 SCRAMBLED CITIES
1. Paris FRANCE
2. Amsterdam NETHERLANDS
3. Berlin GERMANY
4. Canberra AUSTRALIA
5. Washington DC US
6. Rome ITALY
7. Wellington NEW ZEALAND
8. New Delhi INDIA
9. Madrid SPAIN
10. Beijing CHINA
11. Buenos Aires ARGENTINA

P9 GRANDMA'S BIRTHDAY!
Maya rows the boat to Grandma's house with the dog and leaves it there. She rows back and picks up the cat. She takes the cat to Grandma's house, leaves it there, picks up the dog, and takes it back. She swaps the dog for the cake and takes the cake to the island to leave with the cat. Maya rows back with an empty boat, picks up the dog, and takes it back to Grandma's house.

P10-11 READY FOR TAKE-OFF?

```
S H E S E C U R I T Y B M Q X G
E E N S S C H E C K I N L P Z L
R L S W A T D R L A N I M R E T
U I K H L C N M C W D R N R N R
T C W N O B T A J G Q V A T W Y
R O N Z T P R I R W A C I P Y D
A P L X W O S D U U K T N X T Q
P T R D U T R T Y S A B E S A L
E E Q S X R M R A G D T L R B T
D R E D G O K H B G T A S V N Z
M L K D D P K R D V T K E J N
P N M R Y S J D U I R T Y M R D
L V R N D S T R R N O R R M B R
A G L T L A Q R Q L R D T Z M L
N L N J W P A M I B Q A J N M T
E W T B A C K P A C K D Y Y T Q
```

P12-13 SAY WHAT YOU SEE!
1. Inside out
2. Raining cats and dogs
3. Bend over backwards
4. Fast track
5. Turn around
6. Read between the lines
7. Look before you leap
8. Night on the town
9. In a spin
10. Star jump
11. A cut above the rest
12. Moving home
13. Back door
14. Upside down
15. Misunderstood
16. Beat around the bush
17. Breakfast

P14-15 MORSE MADNESS
1. The plane leaves at 12 P.M.
2. Meet me in Rome.
3. Have a great trip.
4. What is your name?

P16 NUMBERS UP!
1. 11, 13, 15 (+2)
2. 51, 61, 71 (+10)
3. 26, 31, 36 (+5)
4. 16, 22, 29 (+5, +6, +7)
5. 14, 8, 1 (-5, -6, -7)
6. hexagon, heptagon, octagon (6-sided, 7-sided, 8-sided)
7. 13, 21, 34 (each number is the sum of the two numbers preceding it)
8. 96, 192, 384 (x2)
9. 22, 15, 8 (-7)
10. 243, 729, 2187 (x3)

P17 MATH MAYHEM

Top ten!

1 + 9 = 10
2 + 8 = 10
3 + 7 = 10
4 + 6 = 10
5 + 5 = 10
6 + 4 = 10
7 + 3 = 10
8 + 2 = 10
9 + 1 = 10

Twenty-one!

0 + 21 = 21
1 + 20 = 21
2 + 19 = 21
3 + 18 = 21
4 + 17 = 21
5 + 16 = 21
6 + 15 = 21
7 + 14 = 21
8 + 13 = 21
9 + 12 = 21
10 + 11 = 21
11 + 10 = 21
12 + 9 = 21
13 + 8 = 21
14 + 7 = 21
15 + 6 = 21
16 + 5 = 21
17 + 4 = 21
18 + 3 = 21
19 + 2 = 21
20 + 1 = 21
21 + 0 = 21

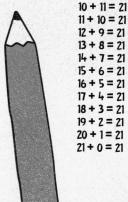

P18 SPIN THE WHEEL

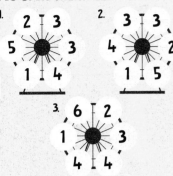

1.
```
  2   3
5       3
  1   4
```
2.
```
  3   3
4       2
  1   5
```
3.
```
  6   2
1       3
  4   4
```

P19 MIND-BENDERS

WHO'S SPEAKING?: Johnny!

R.I.P.: Because if he's living, he can't be dead!

HERE COMES THE BRIDE!: If her husband is a widower, then she must be dead!

BUCKETLOADS: He fills up the 3-gallon bucket and pours it into the 5-gallon bucket. He fills up the 3-gallon bucket again and fills up the 5-gallon bucket (by adding another 2 gallons). What's left in the 3-gallon bucket must be 1 gallon.

P20 FLAGTASTIC

1. Turkey
2. Wales
3. Canada
4. South Africa
5. Kenya
6. Nepal
7. Brazil
8. Japan
9. Switzerland
10. New Zealand

P22 NO SUCH PLACE

Spiderman doesn't exist, but there is a town in Turkey called Batman! All the others really exist.

P23 POLE POSITION

If you pass the car in second place, that puts you in second place. You can't pass the last person, otherwise you'd be last.

P24-25 AIRPORT SUDOKU

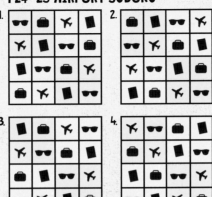

P26-27 FLAG FINDER

1. Look behind you.
2. Can you wave back?
3. What is your name?

P28-29 BIG-CITY QUIZ

La Paz is the world's highest capital city.

Sydney is home to a famous opera house.

Kathmandu is a city in the Himalayas.

Tokyo is close to Mt. Fuji and is the world's biggest city.

The Great Fire of 1666 happened in London.

Day of the Dead celebrations take place in Mexico City.

Cape Town is home to Table Mountain.

Beijing is home to the Forbidden City.

French is spoken in Montreal.

The Seine is a river that runs through Paris.

New York used to be called New Amsterdam AND is sometimes called the Big Apple.

P30-31 DOT TO DAKOTA

Mount Rushmore

P32-33 FAMOUS PLACES

1. Grand Canyon
2. Tower of London
3. Times Square
4. Eiffel Tower
5. Big Ben
6. Great Wall of China
7. Sydney Harbour Bridge
8. Great Pyramid of Giza
9. Leaning Tower of Pisa
10. Leicester Square
11. Marble Arch
12. Mt. Kilimanjaro
13. Victoria Falls
14. Table Mountain

P34 ALL SQUARE

24

P35 PUZZLE IN PIECES

A

P36-37 THE CURSE OF THE PYRAMIDS

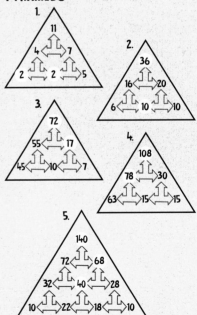

1.
```
      11
    4    7
  2    2    5
```
2.
```
      36
   16    20
  6   10   10
```
3.
```
      72
   55    17
  45   10   7
```
4.
```
      108
    78    30
   63   15   15
```
5.
```
        140
      72    68
    32   40   28
  10   22   18   10
```

ANSWERS

P38–39 RIDDLES OF THE SPHINX
1. Your shadow
2. A needle
3. A teapot
4. An umbrella
5. A ruler (or a tape measure)
6. A pair of glasses
7. An armchair
8. A hole
9. A lettuce
10. A bank

P40–41 IT'S NO PICNIC!

1.

2.
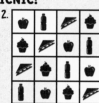

3.
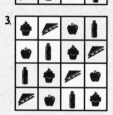

4.
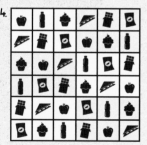

P42 BUREAU DE CHANGE
€20 = $35 CAD (C)
You can buy 3 moose mugs
You can buy 2 bottles of syrup
$75 CAD = €50 (B)
You can buy 10 Eiffel Tower snow globes
You can buy 5 boxes of chocolates.

P43 ALL SPENT
Thailand Baht
United Kingdom Pound sterling
France Euro
US Dollar
India Rupee
Norway Krone
Ireland Euro
Malaysia Ringgit
Japan Yen
China Yuan
Turkey Lira
South Africa Rand

P44–45 LOST IN THE DARK!

P46–47 HIT THE HIGHWAY!
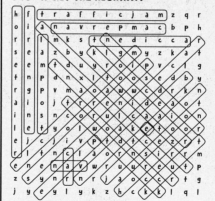

P48–49 WHEEL OF FORTUNE
1. I spy with my little eye.
2. I'm going around in circles.
3. Honesty is the best policy.
4. What is your name?

P50–51 WARNING – HAZARD AHEAD!
1. Neither. Nine and nine are eighteen.
2. Jousted wonder = just one word.
3. Tuesday, Thursday, today, and, tomorrow
4. Not one. None of these animals can talk.
5. The name of the pilot is the name of whoever is reading the story as it says, "I was flying a plane."
6. A butterfly has six legs. Calling its antennae legs doesn't make them legs.
7. The match
8. Four: one green, one pink, one orange, and one blue
9. Your name
10. A hole
11. One. There is only one *m* in "my sentence."
12. Silence
13. Wouldn't you prefer the snake to bite the tiger rather than you?
14. None. Cockerels do not lay eggs.

P52 WORD SCRAMBLE
1. Leek & lettuce (the only vegetables)
2. Ostrich & penguin (neither can fly)
3. Sharpener & ruler (not writing implements)
4. Amsterdam & Madrid (cities, not countries)
5. Happy & content (positive emotions)

P53 AMUSEMENT PARK ATTRACTION

Some of the words you could make are:

LOG FLUME: Mogul, gulf, mole, fell, glue, fuel, glum...

CAROUSEL: Cares, cars, close, coals, coral, euros, laces, louse, oars, race...

HOT DOGS: Dogs, dots, ghost, goods, hogs, hood, host, shot, stood...

BUMPER CARS: Camper, scare, beam, cape, ramp, crumb, sure...

...and lots more! Look again at p53 and see how many more you can find!

P54–55 SAFARI CROSSWORD

P56 WHERE ON EARTH?
North America: I, J
Europe: B, C, N
Asia: D, H, O
South America: F, G, M
Africa: A, E, P
Oceania: K, L

Antarctica is the 7th continent.

P58 STILL IN THE BAG...
Sunglasses, guidebook, necklace, headphones, pack of cards, and dice are all missing. Handle of suitcase is broken.

P59 NAME THAT HABITAT
1. Underground cave
2. Rainforest
3. Outer space
4. Waterfall
5. Wetland
6. Rock pool
7. Deep sea
8. Treeline
9. Arctic Circle

P60–61 UNDERSEA SCRAMBLE
Collected letters: SEURARET, which spells TREASURE

P62 SPORTING SAY WHAT YOU SEE!
1. Tennis (ten x nis)
2. Downhill skiing
3. Soccer
4. Cross-country skiing
5. Long jump
6. 100 meters
7. Curling
8. Abseiling
9. Mountain climbing
10. Synchronized swimming
11. Triple jump
12. High jump

Brain Workout: Maisie is 15.

P64–65 WHERE AM I?
1.
My third is in pain but not in pin. (A)
My second is fourth in can't. (T)
My first is third in slide. (I)
My last is third in why. (Y)
My fourth appears twice in fallen. (L)
ITALY

2.
My first three are what happen when you can't not. (can)
My fourth and my sixth are the same as my second. (A)
My fifth is in bed and also in and. (D)
CANADA

3.
My sixth is first in last. (L)
My second is in pray but not in pay. (R)
My first is in able but not in ale. (B)
My third and fourth begin the alphabet and close it out. (AZ)
My fifth is second in pin. (I)
BRAZIL

4.
My third comes second in ideas but first in dreams. (D)
My first two are at the center of things. (IN)
My fourth echoes my first and comes before am. (I)
My last is in hail but not in hill. (A)
INDIA

P66 THE TAJ MAHAL
B and H match.

P67 THE TAJ MAHAL MISHAP
B, C, D, E, and F

P68–69 CRAZY BAGGAGE CAROUSEL
Abigail = 6
Mohamed = 10
Hui = 4
Linnea = 1

P70–71 TANGLED CHUTES
A = 3
B = 1
C = 4
D = 2

P72 THEY DO THAT THERE?
There is no officially organized sand-throwing festival in Dubai.

P73 DANCING PARTNERS
1) Argentina – b) Tango
2) Austria – f) Waltz
3) Hawaii – d) Hula
4) Brazil – c) Samba
5) Spain – a) Flamenco
6) Scotland – e) Highland dancing

P74–75 ROLL THE DICE
1. Tree
2. Leaf
3. Rock

P76–77 MATCH PLAY

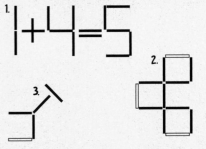

ANSWERS

P78–79 RUNE READER
1. Are we nearly there yet?
2. Runes totally rock
3. Back to the Stone Age
4. What is your name?

P80 MOVING HOME

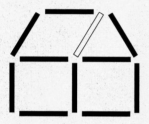

P81 DESERT ISLAND SUDOKU

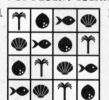

P82 SWING THROUGH THE THREES

It's a monkey

P84 BEACH–BAG MIX UP
Missing: 1 set of goggles, a book, playing cards, and a water bottle. A frisbee and a ball have appeared.

P85 TRICKY TRIANGLES
A 8
B 44

P86–87 AMUSEMENT PARK FUN!

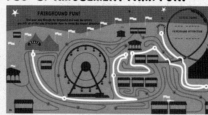

Collected letters: GOLLFMUE, which spells LOG FLUME

P88–89 THINKING CAPS ON!
1. Tricycle
2. One to one
3. Jack-in-the-box
4. Tickets
5. Lost for words
6. Stuck in traffic
7. Backpack
8. Crossroads
9. Lost and found
10. Between you and me
11. On top of the world
12. 6 feet underground
13. Around the world

P90–91 BLINDING BLIZZARD

It's a penguin.

P92–93 PASSPORT PHOTO MYSTERY
Harrison: B
Jacob: G
James: I
David: H

P94–95 AROUND–THE–WORLD RIDDLES
1. A border
2. A map
3. The letter e
4. A towel
5. Footsteps
6. Because polar bears live at the North Pole and penguins live at the South Pole
7. A river
8. A boat's anchor
9. A stamp
10. They both weigh the same

P96–97 LOOKING FOR WILDLIFE
1. Starfish
2. Butterfly
3. Reindeer
4. Duck
5. Tiger
6. Falcon
7. Stick insect
8. Three little pigs
9. Great white shark
10. Polar bear
11. Octopus
12. Toucan
13. Three blind mice
14. Walrus

P98–99 BE AN ARCTIC EXPLORER!

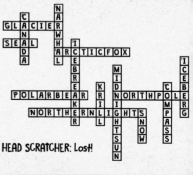

HEAD SCRATCHER: Lost!

P100–101 TREASURE ISLAND

P102–103 HIEROGLYPHS
1. Watch out for the mummy.
2. What music do mummies love? Wrap!

P104 MUDDLED MONUMENTS
Sydney Harbour, Australia
Tower of London, United Kingdom
Statue of Liberty, US
Colosseum, Italy
Taj Mahal, India
Great Wall, China
Red Square, Russia
Parthenon, Greece
Pyramids, Egypt

P105 SORT THE SOUVENIRS
B contains all the pieces

P106–107 SCORCHING HOT!

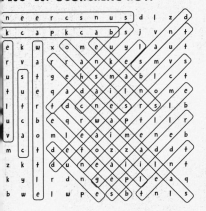

P108–109 PICTURE PLACES
1. Eye, ran = Iran
2. Four ants = France
3. Bell eees = Belize
4. Tennis e = Tennessee
5. Bell gem = Belgium
6. Chili = Chile
7. Cow weight = Kuwait
8. Turkey = Turkey

P110–111 IN THE LOOP
James and Chantal like exactly the same three
activities and are most likely to have a fun
time together.

P112–113 VACATION TIME?
Joe is going on July 16.

1. If Tobias was told that the date is the 18th
or 19th, then he would know the date, as
there is only one 18th and one 19th option. So
Olivia deduces that it isn't the 18th or 19th.
Olivia was given the months, so she must not
have been given May or June – otherwise she
would not be able to discount May and June.
2. Olivia and Tobias know it's not the 18th or
19th, and neither is it May or June.
3. Now Tobias says he knows! The possibilities
are July 14 and August 14, or August 15, July
16, and August 17. So it can't be July 14 and
August, otherwise, he still wouldn't know.
4. Cross off July 14 and August 14.
5. This leaves Olivia with July 16 and August
15 and 17.
6. Olivia says she now knows. She wouldn't
know if it were August 15 or 17, which only
leaves July 16!

P114 NOW YOU SEE IT

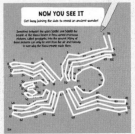

P115 TRICKY TALES!
1. The horse was called Tuesday.
2. An egg
3. He only slept at night.
4. They both weigh the same.
5. They were grandfather, father, and son.
6. You took three, so you have three.
7. He fell off the bottom step.

P116–117 IT'S ALL GREEK
Triangles: 3
Squares: 16
Rectangles: 20

P118 MENU MADNESS
Sushi, Japan
Moussaka, Greece
Adobo, Philippines
Haggis, Scotland
Hamburger, US
Poutine, Canada
Jollof rice, Ghana
Roast beef, England
Goulash, Hungary
Irish stew, Ireland
Ackee and saltfish, Jamaica
Spaghetti, Italy
Pad thai, Thailand

P119 FUNKY FOOD?
Dulce de batte isn't a real dish.

P120–121 IN THE DEEP END
1. Mt. Everest
2. Its name is What.
3. A sponge
4. A breath
5. T, S (they are the first letters of the next
words in the question)
6. Six
7. The soldier in uniform is the boy's mother.
8. A fire
9. A palm tree
10. A cold

ANSWERS

P122–123 SCORCHING SEQUENCES!
1. A (each letter is the first for each month of the year)
2. C (each country's first letter spells the word "blank")
3. C (heading in a west–to–east direction)
4. B (the letters are the first letter of each color in a rainbow)
5. A (nine, ten, eleven)

P124–125 BUSY BEACH

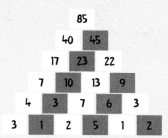

Scrambled letters: WRYBARTERS, spells STRAWBERRY

P126–127 MONSTER MYSTERIES
1. Buried alive
2. Bigfoot
3. The Undead
4. Headless Horseman
5. Raising the dead
6. Wicked Witch of the West
7. Over my dead body
8. Blood is thicker than water.
9. Friday the 13th

P128–129 PERFECT PAIR
10 & 15

P130 PYRAMID PILEUP

			85			
		40	45			
	17	23	22			
7	10	13	9			
4	3	7	6	3		
3	1	2	5	1	2	

P131 SECRET OF THE SPHINX

S	H	X	I	N	P
X	N	S	P	H	I
I	P	N	H	X	S
H	S	P	X	I	N
N	X	I	S	P	H
P	I	H	N	S	X

P132 SQUARED UP
11

P133 IN THE BOX
The pieces in box D form a square.

P134–135 CAMPSITE CAPER
Anaya: K
Matilda: E
Hector: R
Sebastian: F

P136–137 CAMPSITE SUDOKU

1.
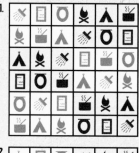

2.

P138–139 LOST IN THE RAINFOREST

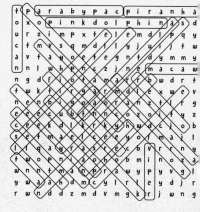

P140–141 MONEY MATTERS
$1 x 15
25c x 10
10c x 5
5c x 11
Total: $23.50

P142–143 BIG-CITY CROSSWORD

P144–145 HOW WAS YOUR JOURNEY?
Karl travels by plane and has a turkey sandwich.
Rosa travels by train and has a cheese sandwich.
Ian travels by car and has a tuna sandwich.
Bert travels by boat and has an avocado sandwich.

P146 LOST HABITATS

1. Tundra
2. Ocean
3. Desert
4. Forest

P147 SUPER-SHAPE SUDOKU

P148–149 DITLOIDS

1. 7 days in a week
2. 7 colors of the rainbow
3. 7 continents on Earth
4. 60 seconds in a minute
5. 60 minutes in an hour
6. 24 hours in a day
7. 8 planets in the Solar System
8. 52 cards in a pack
9. 12 months in a year
10. 26 letters in the alphabet
11. 5 fingers on a hand
12. 2 wheels on a bicycle
13. 3 wheels on a tricycle
14. 4 wheels on a car
15. 6 sides on a die
16. 366 days in a leap year
17. 100 years in a century
18. 12 inches in a foot
19. 10 toes on your two feet
20. 360 degrees in a circle

P150–151 AT THE AMUSEMENT PARK

Annie had a chocolate ice cream and went on the bumper cars.
Leo had an orange ice cream and went on the carousel.
Lily had a pistachio ice cream and went on the ghost train.
Teddy had a strawberry ice cream and went on the roller-coaster.